IT'S NOT ABOUT ME

A ROLLERCOASTER OF EMOTIONS AND LIFE LESSONS FOR ALL TO LEARN FROM

by Christopher M. Milo

It's Not About Me
A Roller Coaster Of Emotions And Life Lessons For All To Learn From
by Christopher M. Milo

Printed in the United States of America.

ISBN 9781498484039

www.xulonpress.com

This book is dedicated to anyone
who has struggled in their life,
with the feeling of being trapped with no way out.
To my God and Savior,
I thank you for being my all and everything.
I give you all the glory, honor and praise.

Introduction

For me, "bullying" has happened repeatedly throughout my life. As the old cliché goes, if you get hit with a lemon, it's time to make lemonade. Keep this in mind as you read my compelling story. It is my hope that it will enrich your life and provide lessons that you, the reader, may take away and apply.

For the record, I believe the word "bully" should be omitted from the English language. I hope to one day see it used in its original seventeenth-century meaning. We'll get to that later.

Over the years, I have learned that the hurtful and harmful feelings we experience as young children are difficult to erase. There is a place in our brain where feelings and emotions are stored called the **hippocampus.** (It is a small organ located within the brain's medial temporal lobe and forms an important part of the limbic system, the region that regulates emotions. The **hippocampus** is associated mainly with memory, in particular long-term memory.)

As we age, we can quickly retreat back to that emotion or pain we once experienced and seemingly bring it back to life. This is similar to how I developed much of the text in this book.

As I researched information on the brain and where our feelings are stored, I came across another piece of information that I thought was interesting. I learned on the University of Rochester Medical Center's web site that teens' brains aren't fully developed; in fact, they're very different from adult brains. Adult brains operate from the prefrontal cortex, the brain's rational part, and teens and children process through the amygdaloid, the emotional part.

Reading this information, one could say that it makes sense why we, as children, become so affected by our younger years. As children, we cannot process things rationally and emotionally like an adult can. I'll leave the rest to the scholars in the medical field.

One thing I ask while you read this book is to never think I was ever the victim. This is a big difference from many self-help books. This is simply a reflection on my life's experiences. I express my feelings and use my early experiences as a tool, to explain my past and hopefully affect you the reader and as many lives that God gives me access to.

These many shared life lessons should provide encouragement. Take a self-inventory and seek what is most important in your life. What is your purpose? What is your life's goal? What are you being called to do? This book is written to help answer these questions.

Once you finish the book, you'll feel confident, with a new perspective on life, looking at things in a new light. This light is unique in each one of us, offering a choice to either share with others or let it fade into a lost and unhappy darkness. I am going to give you simple and realistic solutions to help prepare you for life, regardless of your age.

"13 Messages from Milo" is an easy-to-learn step-by-step process that will help make your life become aligned and your thoughts more in tune to helping others. It will take the focus off self-absorption and will begin to reprogram your thoughts. You'll begin to experience being the light in someone else's life.

Everyone understands that what we are is an assemblage of all the choices we make. When you're reading this book, try putting yourself in the shoes of either side of the many scenarios. For parents, think about how this could potentially impact your child. For students, consider what your teachers and parents must be going through as you read each scenario. Get ready, because your life is about to change. I'm extremely excited for you, as you'll soon enjoy a fresh perspective, a new vision, and a new goal, all to lead you into a new dream for your life. My passion is for you, from this moment forward, to have the tools necessary to make better choices.

Are you ready to begin?

Preface

I wake up most days to a hot cup of coffee or protein drink. I eat breakfast on the road or sometimes sitting at the kitchen table. It's always dictated by where I have to be. If life has kept me at home in the morning, it isn't uncommon for me to look outside between sips and thank God for everything he has given me.

I do my best to hide my phone and forget about it whenever possible, which is really difficult to do when one of my first questions each morning is, "What is the temperature supposed to be?" So, of course, I remember where I hid my phone and I search the local weather and then…it starts!

When I've drunk half my coffee I see all the little alerts at the top of my phone. Between emails, texts and all of social media, some days there are hundreds of alerts.

"What can I dismiss?" is usually my first question. Not long after this, I see a post on social media from a middle school student talking smack about a teacher in their school. I see news about a drunk driver who hit an innocent family of five, where only the two-year-old daughter survived. Two of the first emails I read are from parents reaching out to me about their child who has some type of issue with cutting or self-harm, or they're seeking direction on how to handle a suicide attempt, followed by another from a student telling me he punched another kid and felt bad about it.

How did each of these scenarios carry out to this point? Who do you reach out for guidance or a helping hand? How do kids and parents deal with life's circumstances? Why does this happen to so many families? All of these questions and more will be addressed as you read this book. I've only gotten through two emails and my coffee is already cold.

Table of Contents

one

Grades 1-8

Sometimes you just need to stop what you are doing, eat a
piece of cheesecake, and thank God for that moment.
—*Christopher Milo*

I grew up in a small town about 15 miles west of Akron, Ohio called Wadsworth. It's a beautiful small community where everyone knows everybody. I lived on the north end of Route 261, and I can still smell the sweet aroma of the white flowering trees that stood strong as you drove down my road. The most exciting thing I did as a child was to walk to Great Oaks to see a movie at one of the two cinemas. Walking from my house, we had to cross Route 94, where the traffic was always very busy. When I wasn't feeling so adventurous, it was always fun to take a short walk to Danny's Marathon gas station, where there were always lots of candy and cold drinks.

During the summer, I remember walking to the corner of our road, which was three houses away, and turning left to get to the cornfield to play. Being in the first few years of school, first through fourth grade, I always thought it was cool to be able to walk that far without my parents. As an adult, I realize I can throw a rock that same distance, but back then, it seemed miles and miles away to me. When I was old enough to ride my bike, my parents gave me permission to ride to piano lessons on Saturday mornings. It was only two blocks away, but it felt like I was riding two hundred miles at the time. Jane Ross was one of the eleven music teachers I have had. She made me practice for thirty minutes every day. I remember taking a red plastic toy tomahawk and beating the keys of the piano when I didn't want to practice; that seemed to be a regular occurrence since I never wanted to practice. My parents made me play, and as I look back, I'm grateful that they never gave up on me. I never thought I could make anything of my music, especially since the kids at school gave me so much trouble.

I'm the youngest of three kids. My sister Michelle is eight years older and my brother John is five years older. Being the baby in the family had its benefits! All I had to do was say, "I'm telling," when either of my siblings were misbehaving and the world was my oyster! My brother and sister used to get so mad at me for saying that. We fought over the most ridiculous things. Many times I wished I never had a brother or a sister. For many years, my siblings told me I was adopted and I believed them! It wasn't until I was about twelve years old that the truth came out. I learned that I was in fact a blood member of the family. Our family always joked around so I chalked that one up as one of the longest jokes in history! I always looked up to my brother John. He is a strong man who didn't take anything from anyone. He was the solid one and very driven.

My sister used to take me everywhere with her. I always used to feel like a "big shot" because I used to do high school things with her like going to sporting events and shopping with her friends. It was pretty cool growing up in a small town; however, I wasn't very prepared for what I was about to learn.

Being in grade school was not easy for me. I was picked on for several reasons and experienced what we know in today's society as bullying. One of those reasons, if you can believe it, was that I was always polite and kind to others. The kids used to call me names for that. They said I was a "brown noser," which never made much sense to me. Moreover, it hurt. I was taught to respect others and be obedient. I often thought, "Just because I wasn't raised a certain way or just because I didn't have really nice shoes, doesn't make someone better or worse than me. Am I wrong?"

I went to a Catholic school called Sacred Heart from first through eighth grade. It was different for me because the few friends I had went to public school. They didn't have religion class, they didn't pray in school, and I only had about twenty-five students in my class at any given time throughout the year. I spent eight years with the majority of those same students. By the time we got to the eighth grade, it was like I went to school with my brothers and sisters instead of classmates.

I didn't have many friends in school. I was always the different one, the outcast, the one that nobody wanted to pay any attention to. My favorite time of day at school was lunch. As I reflect, I think it was the most fun for three reasons. First, it got everyone away from me who didn't like me or want to be around me. Second, there was a piano in the cafeteria, and third, I love food!

I started taking piano lessons at the age of five. In school, all I wanted to do at lunch was eat and show my classmates what I had learned from the last week of piano lessons. I would eat my lunch really fast and head over to the piano to play. As soon as I sat down on the piano bench to play, I would look behind me to see if I had everyone's attention. The only thing I saw was a cafeteria full of empty chairs. They all left me and went to recess.

This happened for years. It hurt my feelings so much. Has something like that ever happened to you?

One afternoon, the lunch monitor, Mrs. Pape, saw the disappointment on my face. She said to me, "Christopher, you just keep playing that piano and one day, people all over the world will want to listen to you." Just for the record, I was horrible!

I understand why they didn't want to hang around and listen, but it still hurt to know that I didn't have any support from my so-called friends.

This went on for most of elementary and middle school. On top of nobody wanting to listen to my music, I was horrible at most of the playground activities. I couldn't throw a ball to save my life, kicking a ball was barely an option, and running? Forget about it! As a result, I was always picked last for everything, including playground teams. It was very hurtful! I often found myself alone on the playground. We had a huge tire on the playground, and the bottom half of the tire was below the dirt. The other half was aboveground so kids could climb on it. If you crawled in the middle of the tire, you could climb to the top on the inside. This is where I used to hide from the kids during most of recess. I can remember doing this for many years. I figured no one could call me any names if they couldn't see me.

What was going on with me? I guess I was just a little behind and didn't advance as quickly as other students did. Or was it the other kids?

During the summer before my eighth-grade year, I started playing soccer. I learned how to kick a ball and realized that I was pretty good at it. Now, we had gym class once a week. One afternoon at gym class, we were playing kickball in the church basement. As always, I was picked last for the team— or maybe no one even called my name. Home plate was by the main entrance door of the basement. It was scary-looking. The door was a fifteen-light door, the kind of door that has wood strips going up, down and side to side. In the middle of the door, chicken wire was sandwiched between 2 layers of glass. This is how door companies made security doors years ago. It made the door stronger and also helped to keep the bad guys out.

It was my turn to kick the ball. This time, I knew what I was doing since I had played soccer over the summer break. I had never been chosen to play kickball on a playground team that year, so no one knew I could kick the ball. The score was tied 2-2 and gym class was almost over. There was nobody on base. This was my moment! I could feel the victory and had visions of stepping on home plate with a win.

I kicked the ball so hard that it bounced off the opposite wall. I ran to first base as fast as my legs could take me. The other team hadn't even gotten the ball as I rounded second base. Out of the corner of my eye I could see that someone was getting ready to throw the ball at me as I rounded third base. All anyone had to do was hit me with that red rubber ball and I was out. I looked over my left shoulder and saw the ball coming at me like a rocket. I started to think that this would be another chance for one of my classmates to embarrass me. I was running so fast and jumped as high as I could to miss the ball being thrown at me. The only problem was...

I was only a few feet from the scary door where home plate was. When I came down, my feet hit the ground and the rest of my body went into the glass door! It was awful! I put my hands up to block my face as my left hand and arm went through the glass door. Remember the chicken wire I told you about? I pulled my arm back out from the other side of the door and the remaining glass cut the top of my forearm in two places. I was bleeding everywhere. I will never forget Jim T., one of my classmates. He ran over to me as fast as he could and put both of his hands around my wrist to help stop the bleeding. I thank God for his medical training.

Thirteen stitches later, I became the coolest kid in class! Guess why? Even during the chaos, I still landed on home plate and won the game! Although it was not the victory I had seen in my head, it was still a victory. I never thought winning could hurt so bad.

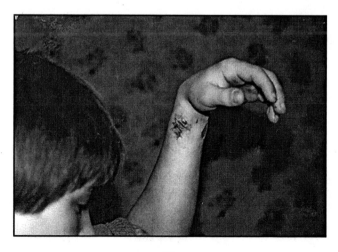

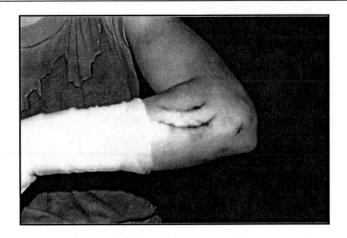

Every time I look at my left wrist I think of the day
it happened.

Have you ever known a fellow classmate like me? If so, be kind to them. **BE POSITIVE** and tell them they will eventually do better and improve what they are trying to do. Keep encouraging them and don't just leave them alone. Include all kids in every activity you do and offer to help them with the things they struggle with. Not everybody advances the same in every activity.

If you change the way you treat others, everything in your life will also change. Everyone wants to be a part of something. Everyone wants a purpose, and everyone I have ever met wants to be loved. Speak from your heart when you speak to others, and do everything you can to be positive in every situation.

We must show love to receive love. When the kids in my class went to recess, every time they knew I wanted them to listen to my music at lunch, was there anything positive about that? No. When we try to be positive, positive experiences will happen. Motivate yourself and others to do great things in life. Life is short and precious, so let's make it a great life together! One person can make a difference in the eyes of someone else. Are you that difference?

Ask a trusted adult or friend to help you with this next section.

- What are two things you can do to reprogram your mind to think more positively? _____

  _____

  _____

  _____

  _____

- Who is one person you know who needs a friend or needs inspiration? _____

- What can you do to improve that person's life?

  _____

  _____

  _____

  _____

  _____

  _____

  _____

It only takes one person to do something kind for someone else. You have a choice: to put a smile on someone's face or to make their life miserable. Your kind words, actions and good behavior just might give them a reason not to spend recess hiding in a tire, like I did.

The summer before my eighth grade year

two

<u>High School</u>

I have learned that it isn't in our time, it is in His time.
-Christopher Milo

A re you kidding me right now? I am freaking out! Ok, let me get this straight. I graduated from my 8th grade class with about 25 students. You could fit four of my school buildings in the high school I am now attending. It's the biggest building ever! Is there a map? Do I have to pay tolls here? How many hallways did you say there are? Where's the bathroom? I have a locker with a combination? Did you say there are 350 students in my class?

WHAT?

I would like to offer you some free advice: Go to your orientation!

No.... I didn't go. Let's review something for a moment.

- *I didn't have any friends in school.*
- *I didn't have any play dates growing up.*
- *I didn't have much success in sports or even playground activities...*

...why would I want to go to orientation?

Do you understand what I was thinking? **It was such a big mistake** on my part.

It was a big change going from my little Catholic school to public high school. I felt very lost. Being a freshman was hard enough, but being **me** as a freshman was even harder ...so I thought.

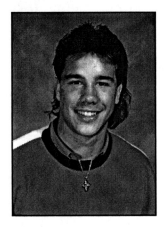

Awesome haircut!

When you go to a new school, there are all kinds of new activities. There was band, choir, Student Council, French and Spanish clubs, and more. What was somebody like me supposed to do to fit in? I decided to do the craziest thing I could ever think of.

I ran for class president!

What was I thinking? I will tell you! I thought things couldn't get any worse for me. I also thought, "What do I have to lose?"

Everyone told me it was just a popularity contest. If that was true, I knew I didn't have a chance. However, I did my own research and learned that the class president's job was to help implement new ideas and programs in the class. I was full of ideas! Most of my ideas were to help other kids in different ways so they wouldn't be treated the way I had been for the last eight years. I passed out fliers reading "Christopher Milo for President." I even hung fliers up in the lunch room and community board in the hallways. Are you ready for this? I won! I was class President for ninth and tenth grades and on Student Council. Would you like to know my secret of winning? I was *positive* in everything I said. I was *genuine*. There wasn't a fake bone in my body. I said what I meant and I meant what I said. I *listened* to the needs of my classmates and did what I could to be an *inspiration* to all. I knew if we *worked together*, *accepted* each other for who we are and *loved* each other with respectful *communication,* we would be well on our way to making a difference in the class of 1990.

The most awesome thing about all of this wasn't the fact that I was the leader of my class. It was the fact that I knew that everything I had to say would be heard by the student body. It was the coolest thing I had ever experienced. I was always used to keeping my opinions to myself, but I found myself being friends with football players, band kids, mean kids, smart kids and even kids from different clubs.

All I wanted was to be *accepted.* I had so much practice trying to make friends. During the previous eight years I had failed, over and over again. Here is what I realized: I was trying to make friends with the same kids for eight years. At my high school, I had a whole new group of kids, more than 300 of them! It was now so much easier to meet new kids.

I found small groups of people in choir and band that seemed to really appreciate my effort with the piano. By the time I was halfway through my ninth-grade year, kids were asking me to play songs in the commons, study hall and choir room. I finally felt like I was somebody! I felt like I mattered. I actually had slivers of feelings that I might just be important! Just being accepted by people was great for me.

The weight room was another place I seemed to find acceptance. Many of the jocks were there, but also many of the kids like me. Kids that wanted to get bigger, feel stronger and build some confidence so as not to get picked on. Even though I'd made more friends and created better relationships with my classmates, there were still those feelings of having to protect myself and keep my guard up.

Perhaps I was just working through the hurt feelings from my previous years, but I'm pleased to report that halfway through high school, the bullying was almost gone. Remember this: no matter where you go and no matter what age you are; it isn't uncommon to find somebody who is going to give you trouble or a hard time for one reason or another.

Many people in our society are so caught up in how we look, how much money we have and making sure we weigh less than other people, while being one step ahead of our neighbors. For me, I just wanted to be *genuine* to people in my school.

I didn't get very good grades in grade school or high school. I wasn't a very prepared student and to be completely honest, I wasn't all that interested in school. I was more interested in my music. I remember it like it was yesterday, taking my school books home and telling my parents I was going to study in my room, where my Yamaha PF2000 digital piano was conveniently located.

I plugged my headphones into my piano, opened the book I was supposed to study, and placed it on top of my piano... but, never looking at a word, I just played the piano for hours. I'm not sure what I was thinking. Maybe the information in the school book placed on the piano would jump into my head and download to my brain? Silly, huh?

I loved that keyboard!

If I could turn back time, I'd definitely pay more attention to my studies and be more focused on learning. A good education is very important for a boatload of reasons. You may not realize it now, but push through the aggravation and homework and work hard. School is your career right now.

Just like your parents go to their places of employment and are doing well, your doing well in school eliminates much of the pressure often experienced in many homes. Do your job, and do it well!

Preschool prepares us for elementary school. Elementary school prepares us for middle school and middle school prepares us for high school, right? Does high school prepare us for life outside of school? I'll get to that later. Here are some important tips.

- Do your work or homework correctly the first time you do it.
- Prepare for each day the night before.
- If you aren't early, you are late.
- If you have a dream, work hard to get your dream.
- Don't be around people who discourage you and say that you can't do something. Surround yourself with those who encourage you instead.
- If you want to play sports in school or participate in clubs, make sure you redeem your time wisely. That's from the good book! (Col. 4:5)
- Write things down! I've always said, if it's not written down, it doesn't exist.
- You will get much farther in life by *listening* instead of talking.
- Use a calendar every day.
- You'll never find someone standing around with a golden ticket that has your name on it. You have to work hard for the things you want.
- If you think you're better than someone else, you may be. However, you don't have to act like you're the only blessing on earth. *Use your talents* to assist those around you, helping them to achieve their goals and dreams. You

31

should see how far I can kick a ball much better now because finally someone helped me.

- Be patient. As a Christian, I have learned that it isn't in our time, it's in His time.
- Don't be lazy.
- Look people in the eye when you speak to them.
- Treat other people as you want to be treated.
- If you don't have something nice to say.... don't say anything at all. (I've heard this my entire life. It shouldn't be anything new to you.)

If you can wrap your head around each of these points, you'll be further along than the person who doesn't; I can practically guarantee it. Let me go back to a question I asked a minute ago.

Does high school prepare us for life outside of school?

The answer should be yes. Most of us are in school for thirteen years, if you include kindergarten. Everything you're learning today, no matter what grade you're in, is preparing you for life. You may choose to further your education and go to college. You may focus on a trade or choose the medical field, adding several more years of school with hands-on training. Either way, everything I have told you applies to all of it.

I used to say to myself, "Why do I need to learn math as a musician? Musicians rarely count past 4!" The truth is, I use math every day on the business end of my music. I have to spell correctly or I'll look like I don't know what I am doing. I have to know how to read or I won't be able to understand the contracts I have to sign.

If you don't manage your time wisely and are often late for appointments and work, it's very likely you'll struggle and possibly put yourself in the position of looking for another job.

Keep the list I gave you for future reference. I had to figure this out on my own. The real challenge is to practice by applying it every day. I believe you can do this!

Maybe I did learn something in school.

I still make the same expression on my
face when I learn that lunch is on its way!

three

Get A Job

You can never check enough times that
the power is off before doing any electrical work.
-Christopher Milo

I didn't graduate high school with honors. I didn't even graduate with a scholarship, but I did graduate. Praise God! After high school, I went to the University of Akron in Akron, Ohio. This decision was heavily influenced by my parents, who always encouraged me to obtain a higher education, music education that is. My parents continued to encourage me to prepare me for what they knew was ahead for me in my life. At least, that's what they hoped for. After one semester of college, I quickly realized that being in a classroom setting was just not for me.

Now what? If I wasn't going to go to full-time school, I guess it was now time to get a big-boy job like the rest of the adults. In high school, I worked at all kinds of places. I remember this place I worked at called Bob's Nursery; it was a great place. Bob, the owner, was always nice and had high expectations. We dug, balled, and burlapped trees, made deliveries, and had many different plants, shrubs and lawn & garden items for sale.

One afternoon, I went to work and there wasn't much to do. I thought it would be a very easy day. I immediately grabbed a broom and started sweeping to keep me busy so I wasn't just standing around. Out of the corner of my eye, I saw Bob walking out of the garage holding a shovel in his right hand. I didn't think much of it until he said to me, "Christopher, thank you for always being on time. I have a special job for you today!" In my mind, I thought this would be the greatest day of my life. Bob obviously saw my value and appreciated me the most out of all of his employees. I was so happy. And I was so wrong!

Bob invited me to walk with him to a building I had never been in. As we got a little closer, I noticed an offensive odor in the air. What could that be? Bob opens the door and BOOM! I almost fell over from the smell. The horse barn smelled like it had never been cleaned out! "You can't be serious," I thought. "This is the appreciation I get for being the best employee?"

No good deed goes unpunished, because for the next four hours, I shoveled horse poop. It was the worst day of my life. Bob did give me a shovel and rubber boots, but they were three sizes too big. With a smile, he said, "All this, (pointing to mountains of poop) needs to be put here (the opposite side of the barn)." I had to put the poop in a wheelbarrow and then dump it on the opposite side of the barn. After three hours of doing this, I thought I was going to pass out. It looked like I hadn't even made a dent. He had to have had at least 500 horses! There was enough poop to fertilize most of the western hemisphere. For the record, Bob only had 3 horses. But it was beyond gross!

What I learned from working at Bob's Nursery was priceless. I learned how to work hard and to respect myself and the work I did. But there was no way I could shovel horse poop the rest of my life, so what was I supposed to do?

In the newspaper, I found an ad in the classifieds for a local lumber company. They were paying good money for people to demolish a section of one of the buildings so it could be remodeled. I was strong and pretty smart, and it sounded easy. I showed up to the interview and remembered everything that I told you I learned in school. I was early for my interview. I was well dressed and very respectful. I looked Rory, the manager, in the eye during my interview and thanked him for giving me the opportunity to meet with him that day. He said, "Christopher Milo, welcome aboard!" I was hired part-time! It was June of 1991 and very warm outside. Inside the building where I was working was about 25 degrees warmer than it was outside.

Some of my many responsibilities included:
- Pulling down walls
- Removing all old wiring in the building

- Driving a forklift (The best part of the job!)
- Throwing trash and debris away in big Dumpsters

The job was extremely demanding and very physical, but I knew I would do anything as long as I didn't have to shovel poop ever again in my life!

I had been working for several weeks at my remodeling career. One afternoon, the guys and I were working on a loft section of the main building. They told me that everything needed to come down and to rip it all out including the walls and the wiring. I took a metal ladder with me so I could reach all the high stuff. I climbed up to the top of the ladder, about 16 feet off the ground. I asked my supervisor, "All this is ready to come down?" He said, "It sure is!" I was speaking of a quad box where you can plug four plugs into the metal box. The outlets were already gone, so I figured it was OK to continue with my demolition. I was so wrong!

I reached into the metal box to pull the wiring out and experienced a sensation like never before. It felt and looked like a Fourth of July party! The 440-volt line wasn't turned off! Part of the joy I experienced included a brilliant flash of light and the rush of air as I flew back. Over 14 feet in the air later I landed. I didn't bounce well, but smashed both my head and shoulder on the not-so-soft ground. My arm had a musty burnt smell and all the guys around me to this day tell me my body was literally smoking for at least 15 minutes.

"Is this for real?" I thought. "I'm lying on the ground, flopping like a fish out of water and smelling like something died. What a great job I have!" (Yes, I am being sarcastic.) I had a headache for a couple of days, but I went back to work anyway.

RULE #1 Always check to make sure the power is off before doing any electrical work. Then check again!

We finished the demo job in about six weeks and the company offered me a full-time job! Over the next several years, I learned everything about residential and commercial construction. It was great to learn the different trades and eventually be able to do much of the work on my own. For the record, I didn't just read an article, show up to an interview and nail it because I was fantastic. I had many little jobs to prepare me for my next steps after high school.

My brother John, sister Michelle and myself.

In high school I had several jobs. I worked:

- At the leather store in Rolling Acres Mall
- At a gift shop at Rolling Acres Mall
- At Bob's Nursery
- Building wooden storage barns
- Playing lots of music shows with bands I was in
- At Johnson Piano Service
- Performing many solo piano gigs

Most of the jobs I had were fun, but some of the best times I had in high school were with my band Power Surge. Looking back, it was a foreshadowing of things to come. Music was my life's dream. Our band was Christopher Milo, singing and playing the keyboard, Bobby Brauer on the bass, Craig Miles on guitar and Brian Nitz on the drums.

(RIP Craig Miles; we love you, brother!)

Lead singer of my band

We thought we were awesome! Just starting out, we were actually pretty good! It was the '80s. We played rock and roll music and experienced everything that came with the '80s. That in itself needs its own book. We played at local clubs and some school events.

While most of my friends were doing high school things, I was always looking for someone to listen to my music. I played everywhere I could in the evening, after school and on the weekends. I did my first real live performance at the piano at the age of 14 at the Tangier Restaurant in Akron, Ohio. I knew about 20 songs at the time. I wrote my first 13-part symphony at the age of 14. Writing music was my passion, but performing was a close second. I played at every nursing home that I could find.

Please allow me to explain.

When I was nine years old, I went to a nursing home in my home town of Wadsworth, Ohio. Even though I was horrible, the elderly people who were listening to me told me to keep playing. They clapped for me. They told me that I would be great and people all over the world would want to listen to my music one day. As I reflect, Mrs. Pape told me the same thing when I was in grade school at Sacred Heart. Hmmm?

I'm not sure my feet even touched the floor!

From sixth grade through my senior year, much of my time after school was spent with Wayne Johnson at Johnson Piano Service. Wayne is a master tuner/technician who has worked on

41

some of the most expensive pianos around the world. We would take the pianos completely apart and put them back together. We would refinish them, restring and tune them. It was a blessing for me to have Wayne as a coach, piano teacher and mentor.

Forgive me for digressing. I learned a craft that is very specialized. The point I want to stress is that I worked hard all through school. I always had a job to pay my bills and never gave up on my musical dreams. Don't rely on your parents and family to hand everything to you, and don't wait for work to come find you. Go look for it. Remember this. You might get several "no's" before you get the "yes" you are looking for, but don't get discouraged and don't give up. You can do anything you put your mind to. You might fail the first ten interviews, but I promise, things will work out to your benefit. Surround yourself with the best people you can find and learn something from each of them. If you're the smartest person in the room, you're in the wrong room. You can learn what to do, or what not to do, from everyone you meet. At least you're taking away something from everyone.

A thought I always had in my mind was that being a piano player and being a construction guy working with saws and nail guns...doesn't mix well.

Allow me to recap. I graduated from high school in 1990. I decided that college was not for me. I was playing music and working at the lumber company. I moved up very quickly to be a manager at the lumber company. I worked very hard, followed everything I told you to do in Chapter 2, and stayed focused. I didn't worry about having girlfriends, going to movies or hanging out with friends. I just worked hard!

Little did I know, life was about to change.

This is how big my hair was in 1990. This picture was taken at my brother's wedding, with my mother, Helen.

four

Life Just Stopped

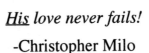

<u>His</u> love never fails!

-Christopher Milo

As a manager at the lumber company, I had many responsibilities. I had to open and close the store, place orders for building materials, inventory products, do payroll and help outside in the lumber yard when needed. Another responsibility I had was to help prepare the deliveries that were going out the next day.

It was the best job yet. I was one of the youngest managers in the company and was perfectly positioned for my own store in the very near future. All I had to do was keep the store neat and clean, meet or exceed my budgets and keep the shelves and the lumber stacks full and ready to sell.

It was November 8th, 1992. I went to work as if it were any other day. I opened the store at 6:30 that morning and Robert, one of my employees, brought doughnuts and coffee for us all to share. I had the best team a company could ask for. It was cold outside and the only heater on the property was inside the office. If you weren't working hard, it was easy to get cold very quickly.

One of my guys said, "Christopher, I'm going outside in the lumber yard to pull the materials for the big house package you sold." I said, "Great, Jim, I'll help you. I sold it, so the least I can do is help you."

Jim started the forklift and moved it to the floor joists. They were 2x10x16's of Southern Yellow Pine. They were heavy, and even heavier when they were wet. Jim pulled the forklift off to one side of the bunk of lumber. I was on the opposite side of the forklift and started grabbing the boards so I could place them on the forks. Jim was at the other end, making sure they were neat and organized. Heavy lifting wasn't new to any of us, but that day helped inspire much of this book.

As I write this, I can still smell the damp lumber and the cold rain on it. I can smell the exhaust from the fork lift we named Bertha. I can see the drips coming through the ceiling of one of the canopies across the yard where some of the lumber was stored.

After about ten minutes of bending over and grabbing the heavy boards, I reached down to grab another board and the worst thing of all happened. I could not stand up. I was stuck in the bent over position with the worst pain you can possibly imagine. My back hurt so bad that it brought tears to my eyes. Jim saw the pain that I was in and called inside the main building to ask for help. No one knew what to do for me and absolutely no one knew what was wrong with me.

The guys rolled my motionless body onto an empty shingle pallet. They fired up the forklift and picked me up and put me in the back of Jim's truck. I would like to remind you that it was November and cold. Everyone was frightened and all anyone wanted to do was get me some help as quickly as possible. Jim quickly found his keys and jumped into his truck and drove out to the main road with me in the back still unable to move. As we entered the highway, I was literally freezing to death. Jim took the truck off the next exit and pulls into what he thought was a doctor's office. Unfortunately, it wasn't the kind of doctor I needed, as it was a chiropractor's office. All the guys took me up to the door, still on the shingle pallet, and put me on the doctor's table while I was still bent over.

Any time a doctor tells you "You may feel a little pressure," you had better buckle up! There I was on my hands and knees, looking like a wrestler in a prone position. This doctor decided to put his hands together and place them in the middle of my back and press straight down…as hard as he could.

I don't remember if there were any sounds because I think my ears stopped working. My guys said that my face was bright red, I was crying and screaming but nothing was coming out of my mouth. It was the worst pain I have ever experienced. The ambulance came to the doctor's office and took me to a local hospital. After X-rays and an MRI (which is a fancy X-ray that takes better pictures), the doctors told me that I had 2 herniated degenerative discs. These discs, located in my lower back, are referred to as the L4 and L5 discs. The bulging discs were pressing against my S1 which is called the sciatic nerve. Because there was an 8.5mm herniation on my L5 disc and a 4.5mm herniation on my L4 disc, I was now paralyzed from the waist down.

If there was ever a time where your life flashes before your eyes, this was it. I had my own apartment off East 185th and Lakeshore in Cleveland, Ohio. I was 20 years old and one of the youngest managers in the company. With everything going my way, I was now paralyzed and unable to walk. On November 8th 1992, I went from "hero to zero" in the blink of an eye, or, as fast as someone can bend over to tie a shoe. I was unable, literally unable, to take care of myself. I had to move out of my apartment and back to my parents' house.

Many doctors worked on my case. The specialists and the doctors said they had never seen an injury as bad as mine in a young man my age. They said they had seen injuries as bad as mine, but in men much older than me. Everything changed and life just stopped.

In the next couple of weeks, I started physical therapy. I had to reprogram my body and my mind to make my legs work. It was horrible. Nothing was going well at all. After several months of not much happening, the doctors started talking to me about a surgery called a microdisectomy. That is when they make a 3" incision in the lower back and go in to trim the herniated discs to try and relieve the pressure from my sciatic nerve.

The docs gave me a 50/50 chance of success: a 50% chance the surgery would work and a 50% chance I would be stuck in a wheel chair for the rest of my life. I was uninterested in odds like that so I said "No thanks!"

I laid in bed and counted the dots on my ceiling for entertainment, a new number coming to mind every time. I would wait till everyone left the house, roll out of bed and crawl down the hallway of my parent's house. They had a full view storm door on the front door. Once I got the front door open, I could prop myself up high enough to see outside through the full view storm door. I didn't get out much. There was nothing I could do. I felt like I was going crazy and all the medication they gave me for inflammation and pain was making me crazier. I stopped taking the medication because it was making me feel weird and sick all the time.

The worst thing about my exhausting crawl down the hallway was passing my piano as I got to the front door. People have asked me what was the worst part about being paralyzed.

It was the fact that I could not sit on my piano bench and play. The piano was my best friend. It never ran outside to recess when I wanted to play it. It never called me any names and it never made fun of me because I couldn't kick a ball. It was as nice to me as I was to it. I felt so lonely. I felt like there was no hope. I had no purpose in my life and all I was to anyone was an inconvenience and a burden.

This was my 21st birthday cake

I celebrated my 21st birthday that March with a music note cake, stuck in a bed that I was growing to really dislike. My entire body hurt from not being able to move and when I did, I was tired very quickly. Winter was gone. Where did it go? My big 21st birthday came and went with no party at all.

Spring was right around the corner. I could see through the blinds of my bedroom window. The leaves were growing back on the trees. I could hear neighbor kids playing outside enjoying the warmer weather, and every day that passed was another day that I wished I had never been born.

It was now May 1993. I was approaching the six-month anniversary of my being paralyzed. I was miserable. I hurt everywhere. I didn't want to leave my room. I was tired of people helping me. The meds hurt my belly and it seemed that nobody wanted to come visit me because they felt bad seeing me in such a condition.

The night of the six-month anniversary of my paralysis, I was crying in my bed, like I did most nights, crying myself to sleep. This night was different. It was different because unlike other nights, I decided to pray.

"God, this can't possibly be what you have planned for me. You've blessed me with so many gifts. Over the years, You've helped me overcome so many things. Why am I still in this bed after six months? If this is what You have planned for me, I'll accept it. I am going to need some help because I'm not doing well on my own with this. I can't visit my friends, I can't work, I can't even sit on the piano bench to play. I can't use the talents that you gave me, Lord.

But God, if you would just give me my legs back, I promise to do something good with my music."

I woke up the next morning feeling no change at all. The disappointment was overwhelming. I was beyond angry and all I wanted was to sleep. That afternoon, I awoke from a nap and for the first time in six months I felt calm and peace unlike anything I have felt before. I said, *"God, is that you?"* and received nothing but silence. Three days after praying that prayer and making that covenant before God, I woke up for my morning crawl to the bathroom. I made it back to bed just hoping I could sleep the day away. My elbows hurt from crawling with my arms and dragging my heavy frame.

But God had a different plan.

This time when I woke up from an early afternoon nap, I stretched out like I had just woken from the best night of sleep ever! I moved my head, my neck, my hands and rolled over. I felt like my left foot was asleep. Let me say that again. *I felt like my left foot was asleep.* You know how it feels fuzzy when your hand or feet fall asleep? I hadn't felt anything below my belly button in six months and three days! After about 30 minutes of me trying not to explode from excitement, I could feel my left knee. I could rotate my left foot. I said, "Thank You, God!"

I had asked for and received my healing! It took about a year and a half of physical therapy, but I now walk to every piano I can find and play it until my fingers can't take any more. I walk just fine now with almost zero pain. I walk, run, play sports and

51

lift weights at the gym. The most awesome thing is that I have never had a surgery.

> *Trust in the Lord with all your heart and lean not*
> *on your own understanding. Acknowledge him*
> *in all your ways and he will direct your path.*
> *—Proverbs 3:5-6*

At the time I was a young baby Christian. I knew enough to give myself to Jesus Christ and build a relationship. What I didn't understand at the time was this. When we pray for something, it doesn't matter what we want and what we think our timing is. That is up to God. We have to be obedient to Him and be patient. His love never fails.

Celebrating Christmas 1992, paralyzed

<u>five</u>

<u>Choices</u>

Welcome all mistakes. Learn from them and don't repeat them.
-Christopher Milo

*E*verything we think, say, and do begins with a single thought. Each one of us has a choice of what to do with that very thought. Let's do a short exercise. I'd like you to write down all the thoughts you have had in the past week. Seems impossible, right? Let's try this. From the time you woke up yesterday to this moment, write down five thoughts that you had. Take your time with this.

1._____

_____

2._____

_____

3._____

_____

4._____

_____

5._____

_____

Now, write down three things you think about all the time.

1._____

_____

2._____

_____

3._____

_____

Now, write down two things you don't like.

1._____

2._____

Do you see any similarities in your answers? Do you see any-thing that sparks your attention? If you remember, in Chapter 1 I spoke of reprogramming your way of thinking. We are now on our way to making different choices that can and will make a huge impact in your everyday life.

Some scholars say that you will have approximately 70,000 thoughts today. According to the National Science Foundation, our brains produce thousands and thousands of thoughts every day, depending on how deep of a thinker you are.

At this point of the exercise it doesn't really matter what five things you thought about. It doesn't matter what three things you think about all the time or what two things you don't like. I wanted to give you some specific directions, so you could revisit your answers in the future and to make you think.

I am going to give you eleven items to think about. I want you to practice thinking about these items every day. If one of the items you wrote in your list is negative, I invite you to use one of my examples to replace it.

1. Today is going to be a great day.
2. I can accomplish anything I want in life.
3. I can replace "what if" with "what could be."
4. Nothing is impossible.
5. Things I have to work hard for are probably worth it.
6. I will never give up on something that I can't go a day without thinking about.
7. It is not our abilities that show what or who we truly are. It is how we choose to use those abilities that helps define who we are.
8. I'll live a life of "oh well" rather than a life of "if onlys." At least I tried.
9. The only thing I see outside these walls is opportunity.

10. I'll welcome all mistakes. I'll learn from them and won't repeat them.

11. I'll read the Bible and pray.

These are just some of the things I try to do every day.

Reprogramming our minds to think in a more positive way leads to a healthier and happier life. I was ready to close all doors when I was paralyzed. The above list is what I practiced to get me through.

I want to continue this lesson while we're on a roll. I'm going to give you two different lists that we will later compare. The first list is for a parent/guardian of the home. The second list is for the child/student in the home. We're going to work together to have a better understanding of each other's thoughts and concerns.

Parents/Guardians:

1. Are you spending quality time with your child? I'm confident that there are some family circumstances that don't allow you to have one-on-one time with your children. I have those too. However, when you're with your children, take a moment to throw the ball, play a game, tell a joke and laugh together or simply give them a hug. It makes me think of my kids when they were about three and six. The gift I got them was in the corner of the room

while they played with the box it came in. You're a gift to your children; now go be the box and have some fun. What are some fun things you can do with your children that maybe you have never done before?

_____

_____

_____

_____

Child/Student

Are you offering to spend time with your parents or guardian? I know the demands of schoolwork and how hard it is to keep up with social media these days. I expect you to put your device down long enough to have a real conversation with the adults in the house. Yes, even if you have to plan it! Try playing a game I played with my kids called high/low. Everyone playing talks about what the best part of their day was and what wasn't so good. This opens the door for everyone to share their day in a fun way. This game should never stop, no matter what age you are! *Be Genuine* and considerate of each other.

_____

_____

_____

_____

_____

Parents/Guardians:

2. Keep the drama out of your life. Work days are not always the best. I get it. Speak to a relative or your spouse. The only thing our children need to hear is positive, uplifting life lessons. Speak life in front of and to your children. It isn't their fault you don't like your job or your boss. Maybe it is time for a change?

_____

_____

_____

_____

Child/Student

I will be the first to say that we parents do not have all the answers. Life does not come with a workbook of how to best conduct our lives. Your parents may need you to be sensitive in certain situations. Remember to be part of the solution instead of the problem.

_____

_____

_____

_____

_____

Parents/Guardians:

3. Stop comparing yourself and family to others. You are choosing to make that important and driving yourself nuts over it. I am certain that there are many people who have less than you do. Be grateful for where you are and what you have. Develop a plan working with your current means to reach higher goals if that is what you desire. Stop beating yourself up.

_____

_____

_____

Child/Student:

I have been to the richest school districts and to some of the poorest. Stop worrying about the shoes someone else is wearing. Stop telling your parents that what you have isn't good enough. Work with your parents on a plan to create goals that will help you both reach your dreams.

The choices you make today will affect you and those around you. Let's reprogram our ways of thinking. *Trust* me. I promise you'll see great results if you stay with this on a daily basis.

Parents/Guardians:

What are some special things I can do each week and month for my children and spouse? _____

_____

_____

_____

_____

_____

_____

_____

_____

_____

Child/Student:

What are some special things I can do each week and month for my siblings and parents?

_____

_____

_____

_____

_____

_____

Quality time with family, in a drama-free, non-comparing environment, with a focus on random acts of kindness, will change you and your family and help you become a healthier person and have a happy family.

I invite you to dissect the statement above. Detail your thoughts in the space provided and come up with solutions for yourself. What does quality time with family mean to you? What do you need to do to create a drama-free environment at home or work? What do you need to stop comparing yourself to? Who do you know that needs a kind word or random act of kindness? It may be the next stranger you meet. What are you going to do for them?

_____

_____

_____

_____

_____

_____

_____

_____

_____

six

Cancer Or Not

I never thought a little act of kindness would impact my life the way it did.

-Christopher Milo

It doesn't matter what we say or do regarding some things, life just seems to take over. Because of my past, cancer has a special place in my heart. Before I got involved with patients of pediatric cancer in the Cleveland, Ohio area, I experienced cancer in my own family. Some of my family got through it and some did not. The point I want to make clear is that I never thought my talents would have a place in the world of those with cancer; however, God had a different plan for me.

I have had the privilege of meeting hundreds of children and adults battling all types of cancer. I have worked with many hospitals around the USA and have met many music therapists. Could I really have a place in all this? Let me explain.

After the agreement that I made to do something good with my music, I continued to play all over the USA and Canada. I played in Las Vegas, New York, Chicago and many of the major cities.

I was playing a song one night in Las Vegas, a rather jazzy number called "When Sunny Gets Blue." I looked around the club to see a room full of well-dressed people. I looked at my tip jar and it was so full, you could not fit another dollar in it. It was at that point that I realized how unhappy I was. Here I was in a Las Vegas nightclub looking at a filled-to-the-brim tip jar, knowing full well that I had made a promise to God, the One who had healed and restored me. I was using this second chance to benefit and glorify myself, not God. That night I got on a plane and left Las Vegas, and it turned out to be one of the best decisions I had ever made.

Doors began to open and I started visiting hospitals. I love kids, since I am one at heart, and I love to play the piano, but why there, why then? I was about to find out. For those of you that have been in children's hospitals, there is always an acoustic piano somewhere. They use the pianos for activities and little concerts. One afternoon, I randomly showed up to Akron Children's Hospital, in Akron, Ohio, knowing there was a piano in the lobby area. I walked up to the lady at the front desk and said, "Hi, my name is Christopher; may I play your piano?" She looked at me up and down and replied with a negative tone of voice, "If you think you can!" I didn't react. I just said, "Thank you."

I sat down at the upright piano, shut my eyes to give Him the glory and began to play. People of all ages started gathering around the piano just staring at me. "What are they thinking?" I asked myself. Still to this day I have no idea what they were thinking, but I knew this. They weren't thinking about cancer. They weren't thinking about diabetes, or blood work, or any other reason they were in the hospital that day.

I looked up to the sky while I was playing and said, "Are you being serious right now?" This can't possibly be where you expect me to play. As clear as you can see yourself in a mirror, I saw the face of God nod, "Yes." I just kept playing and could feel the Holy Spirit deep in my belly. The music I played was beautiful, original and anointed. That's how I know it was not me.

Glory to God.

I am fairly certain that I have had an angel following me around over the years. Think about it for a moment. With all the cuts and bruises, brokenness, paralysis and mental and emotional turmoil, how can it be me that is bringing all of this music to life? I firmly believe, it's not about me.

In my musical career, there have been countless performances around our beautiful country. The important shows are the ones I'd like to speak about. I have performed at over 600 retirement homes, including skilled nursing, memory care and assisted living. I have played in over 150 hospitals and Ronald McDonald houses, as well as countless private concerts for hospice patients. Many of the patients I played for passed away during or shortly after a private concert. In one case, an elderly lady who was a concert pianist in her younger days requested to hear me play live one last time. I took my piano to her room and played at her bedside. She listened to my live private concert and passed away about 20 minutes after I started playing. My music was the last music on earth that she heard. Is there a greater blessing I could be a part of?

In every place around the USA and Canada that I toured, I found a children's hospital to visit the kids and play for them. One stop was in Michigan. I was hired to perform for a large private party. There were hundreds of people waiting to hear my music and later visit with me at the after-party, but all I could think about was this: "Am I really using the talents I was blessed with for the right reasons?" The next day after I woke up and drove back to Ohio. I knew there was a children's hospital in Ann Arbor, Michigan. I went off my direct route and about 25 miles later, I found the hospital. I went straight to the oncology floor and told the people in charge I was there to offer my musical talents and meet some children, to try and put a smile on the young faces. At this moment, I felt like I had a purpose, a much greater purpose than the previous night at the big show.

Walking down the hallway of the oncology floor, I heard a little voice say, "Hey." I took a couple of steps backward and saw a bald little girl in the room all by herself. I looked in the room and said, "Hello." Before I entered the room, I made eye contact with one of the nurses, asking permission to go in. She smiled and whispered, "Go ahead." I went into the room and said, "My name is Christopher. What's your name?" "I'm Monica," she replied. I noticed that next to the bed of this four-year-old little girl were construction paper, glue, scissors and other items used to make crafts. I said, "What are you working on?" She replied, "I am making a craft for my mommy."

Monica had a brain cancer called medulloblastoma. She was making a craft for her mommy before her surgery, which was the very next morning. I said, "May I see your craft?" She handed me the piece of pink construction paper that she had cut out in the shape of a heart. When I opened up the heart, it read,

"I LUVE MY MONMY"

I later found out that when doctors do not think a surgery is going to work out, they encourage these children to create and write cards like this to their loved ones since it may be the last time they will see them. In Monica's case, this was her last chance to try and get rid of the cancer. Monica began to look at me like I was a ghost. Big eyes and tears were ready to pour out of her eyes, but there was no frown on her face. She had no expression on her face from the moment I walked in the room. She said, "Come here," in a gentle whisper. I was about six feet from her bedside but moved closer. She said to me again in her cute little voice, "Come here." I got to the side of her bed and bent down on one knee next to her, and she reached out her hand and gently touched my face. While she was staring at me with her loving little eyes, she reached over to the night stand with her other hand and grabbed the construction paper scissors off the nightstand. She gently grabbed a small section of my hair and began to cut it off. The biggest smile I had ever seen was on this little girl's face. Then another section of my hair was cut off. The smile just kept getting bigger and bigger with each section of hair on the left side of my head. I said, "Are you having fun?" She said, "Yes! I'm going to make you look just like me! So pretty!" I said, "You better do the other side now!" So she did.

So, one afternoon in the summer of 2008 at the children's hospital in Ann Arbor Michigan…I got a haircut from a four-year-old little girl who wanted to make me look as bald as her.

I never thought this little act of kindness would impact my life the way it did. But before I get into that, what was I going to do with my hair—or lack of hair—now?

To correct the new trendy hairstyle I just received from this four-year-old aspiring hairstylist, my first idea was to just shave the sides of my head where Monica had just cut and do a little fade up. That would have been great except that Monica's fabulous hair design was cut higher in some places and lower in others and the only thing I could do was shave the sides completely off. The result was the start of a little mohawk!

I am confident that day was all about Monica. Not me. Not my hair. Nothing that mattered to me was important. I think we're put in unique places to help others get through difficult times. We simply need to be obedient to what we are called to do. I have struggled with being obedient over the years but on this particular day, I **listened**. It wasn't until years later that I understood why.

In 2014, Monica sent me an email telling me that she is now ten years old and cancer free! You can go ahead and cry now. I sure did.

Who do you know that needs something exceptional? What can you do for someone else, without expecting anything in return?

_____

_____

_____

_____

_____

seven

In The Studio

I am convinced that God sent me an angel that night to pro-
vide comfort and take care of my anger and hunger.
-Christopher Milo

L ife on the road and recording in a studio is not always easy. For years I have had the privilege of performing with some of the biggest names in the music industry and with some of the most talented musicians from all over the world.

I'm going to take you back to the Summer of 2007 when I wrote the music for my "Broken Strings" album. Let me remind you, by this time in my life, I had been through multiple multi-million dollar contracts that did not work out, and a lot of co-writing for other bands. I had started a family and had a solid taste of what success and failure really tasted like.

I had worked in studios in many of the big cities, but I am still realizing that my plan is not His plan, and my wanting things *now* isn't in His time for me. So I did what I knew and recruited a dear engineering friend of mine to help me record my album. After some research on home recordings, I made a checklist of everything we needed:

- 3 blankets, to stuff in the windows of my front room
- 4 mattresses, one for each of the 4 walls to help sound-proof the room
- Microphones
- Quarter-inch cords
- Laptop
- Duct tape
- Gaff tape
- Computer and software (and someone who knew how to use a computer!)
- To tune my grand piano
- Extension cords
- A set list of my songs
- Microphone stands

That should do it. Sounds really professional, huh? Not hardly, but I was always taught to use what you have, and at the time, that was the best I could do. I did my research and the hardest part was laying out the room. The music and recording part was easy. Push the button to start recording, I play, then push the button to stop recording. It was that simple.

After being in all the professional studios, I had picked up a lot of tips and used every bit of knowledge I had. We were now ready to hit the space bar. That is "recording talk" for start and stop. I recorded the first song and immediately said, "Let's go to the next one." Ten songs later, one after another, the songs were recorded.

I went to bed that night with my first solo album recorded. No errors. No redo. What we recorded was it. I'm not sure how many thousands were sold but it was not very many. I did the album release party at the Barnes and Noble bookstore in Fairlawn, Ohio. The place was packed. My CD was flying off the shelves. We had an after-party at the Holiday Inn next door. I performed the songs on my album as well as some popular requests. I will never forget that awesome feeling of accomplishment, thanks to a handful of friends, family and Him.

Life on the road is a completely different thing. In a typical short four-week tour, I would contact three or four cities that were close together. This kept my travel expenses down. I would go to Pittsburgh one week, New York the second, Columbus, Ohio the third, and finally Cleveland the fourth. Then it was back home to the Akron area. When you're doing this as a solo musician, most of the tour is scheduled. If you find some down time, it's always good to pop in somewhere and play for tips or fill in for a band.

I would make anywhere from three to six thousand dollars a week doing what I love to do. After expenses and CD sales, it was not uncommon for me to end my month with fifteen to twenty-five hundred dollars. Did you notice the large thousand-dollar gap? You never really know where you're going to end up financially. It's very unpredictable, but I'll tell you this: I wouldn't change it for anything. I met many wonderful people over the years and built many lasting relationships. I also experienced a tremendous amount of disappointment.

One night, I was playing in downtown New York City. I was performing the late shift from nine to midnight. When I was done playing, the manager was supposed to hand me twelve hundred dollars in hundred-dollar bills. For the record, I had done this gig a handful of times. I trusted this all to work out, but this particular night, the manager left before my shift ended. I didn't get paid. I was in serious trouble.

I had about forty-five dollars in my pocket, which resulted in me sleeping in my car that night on the dark streets of NYC. I was so hungry. I needed fuel for my car. If I ate, how would I have enough money to get home? I was scared. I remember it was about 1:45 a.m. I couldn't sleep, because I was getting more scared as the night went on. I started dozing off. The next thing I remember was a knock on my window. I was so startled, I about hit the roof of my car! There was a man outside asking me to roll down my window. What could I do? I rolled down my window and said, "Can I help you?" He said, "It's cold outside, and you're sleeping in your car with no engine running; aren't you cold?" I said, "Yes, and hungry too." He said, "Let's go get dinner." I told the beggar I didn't have any money and he proceeded to say, "You don't need any money where we're going. I know a place with the best burgers in town and they are open twenty-four hours a day."

This guy looked to be about sixty years old and if he had had five bucks to his name, I would have been surprised. He smelled like he hadn't showered for weeks, but I did get a whiff of maybe some cheap cologne. His beard and hairstyle weren't kept up very well.

In the blink of an eye, I was walking down the road with this man. Had I lost my mind? I was in New York walking the streets with a complete stranger, starving and still angry that I hadn't gotten paid!

All of a sudden I had this peace come over me. After two blocks of walking slowly down the road at an ant's pace, I learned that Joe had been in the war years ago and was shot in the leg. He told me a little about his son and daughter and everything he told me was so sweet. He was a kind man and I found myself building a friendship with a stranger that was awesome. We arrived at this burger place he spoke so highly of and found ourselves a seat.

Other than the staff, there were only three people in the place. Immediately when we walked in, we were greeted by a waitress who said, "Good morning, Joe." I thought he must be a regular.

He replied, "Good morning, Kelly." Kelly brought over two coffees and two menus. I remember looking at the clock, which read 2:10 a.m.

I asked Joe if he really gets free food here and he said, "I sure do and so do you." I said, "Nothing is free in this world." He said, "Order what you want."

Two juicy all-beef bacon cheeseburgers, fries, and big fat pickles showed up to our table. Joe ordered the exact same thing that I did. I was convinced he did this because I was getting stuck with the bill. Every thought I had was, "How am I getting home if I am spending money here? I'm in so much trouble."

It was the best burger I had ever eaten. Joe knew his burgers! While we were eating, Joe asked me to share more about myself. I told him my story about what happened that night and not getting paid and what I was doing in New York. He thought it was the coolest thing ever that I played the piano. I told him about my family and what I went through as a little boy. I told him I hoped to record another album one day and that he should come to one of my concerts. He shared stories from the war and more about his life. We both shared our trials, our likes and dislikes.

It was about 4:50 a.m. and I was not sleepy at all. I was having the best time ever. I started to worry about my car being on the road and wanted to get back to it before it got any later. I told Joe I was going to the bathroom to wash my hands. On my way to the bathroom I asked Kelly if she would give me the bill. She said it wasn't necessary. There was no way I was going to let Joe pay for this meal. I made a friend, and the least I could do is buy him dinner.

I finished washing my hands and walked out of the bathroom. Kelly said, "Joe told me to tell you he said goodbye." I was so sad. I knew this had been too good to be true. She handed me the bill, which came to about twenty-five dollars. I had to give the lady a decent tip; she had been serving us coffee for three hours and never rushed us. Being a musician, I know how important tips are. Once again, a peace came over me. I paid the bill, left her a ten-dollar tip, and thanked her repeatedly for her kindness and hospitality. I felt happy to pay the bill and tip her. I felt sick at the same time. If I didn't get paid in the morning, I risked my car getting towed. I couldn't get home with ten dollars, and now I was freaking out.

Kelly said, "So how do you know Joe?" I said, "You mean the guy that left me with the bill?" She chuckled and said, "I told you that you didn't have to pay the bill." I said, "That's okay, I really enjoyed my time with him." She just laughed and said, "If you're hungry, we're open 24 hours a day. What you did was really nice. I overheard you talking with Joe about not having much money to pay the bill, tip me or even get home." I said, "I'm blessed and my music will help get me home...I hope." She replied, "I'm certain you have nothing to worry about, Mr. Piano Man." I said, "Thanks," and walked out the door.

It was now 5:05 a.m. and it was getting brighter outside, with the sun ready to come up. I got back to my car to find a paper under my windshield wiper. Are you kidding me? Getting a ticket was the last thing I needed. When I picked up the ticket, it was not a ticket. It was an envelope and on it was a note from Joe.

It read:

> *Good luck with your next album. Any time you're hungry, just go see my daughter, Kelly, and she will always feed you.*
>
> *Joe*

Inside the envelope there was twenty-five hundred dollars in hundred-dollar bills. I later learned that Joe and his daughter Kelly, who never said a thing, owned six of these burger places in the city. I never saw Joe again, but I am convinced that God sent me an angel that night to provide comfort and take care of my anger and hunger.

I made it home without a care in the world. I saved one of those hundred-dollar bills for years. And when I went back to the studio in 2014, to record the "…thirteen messages" album, I thought about Joe during every track. May God bless him, wherever he is.

eight

The Creation Of The "13 Messages From Milo"

I have made it my mission, my ministry, my life's work to ensure our young learners, parents, and educators are all on the same page.

-Christopher Milo

L ife is full of successes and failures. I have had my share of both. When I think about how the "13 Messages from Milo" came together, it is beautiful, anointed, fascinating and at times, hard for me to comprehend. Once again, I don't consider myself any of these things, which is why I know for a fact that He put this all in place.

People always ask me, "Why 13?" I don't really have an answer that will make you scream, "Holy cats!" but I can tell you this:

- For 13 school days in a row, I was not invited to play one game on the playground.
- "M" is the 13th letter of the alphabet.
- Many people think the number 13 is negative or spooky. I think that is ridiculous.
- I had 13 stitches put in my arm in grade school.
- When I was paralyzed, I used to count by fives, sevens, twelves and thirteens to keep my mind occupied.
- The longest original song I ever recorded was exactly 13 minutes long.
- When I started thinking about all the things I wished were different for me from my childhood, there were 13 character traits that I wished were different in one way or another.

Which brings me to that list. But before I begin, I want to make something very clear. When I was class president in high school, I told you one of the coolest things I experienced was to be heard. I have made it my mission, my ministry, my life's work to ensure our young learners, parents and educators are all on the same page. In my experience, I have learned that a successful school, leadership team, business or home has certain core values and best practices.

It is my belief that if our schools implement and spend more time on the "13 Messages from Milo," students will spend less time posting inappropriate posts on social media, educators will become as focused on "life lessons" as they are on state-mandated requirements, and parents will become more involved and have greater success.

There is an overall, united understanding which cultivates a culture where students, staff and parents look forward to participating. Involvement becomes greater with that understanding, because the environment in which this is implemented becomes a place where nobody wants to leave. People begin to enjoy the company of those around them, because everyone is applying the same awesome traits that make just about everything in life a success. Make sense? I promise it will. Let me show you how simple this is.

Here they are:

Be Positive

Accept

Be Curious

Inspire

Coach

Be Genuine

Work Together

Be Creative

Trust

Communicate

Listen

Use Your Talents

Love One Another

81

nine

Now What?

Is this my ministry? Is this my ultimate purpose?
-Christopher Milo

What am I supposed to do with all of this information? How can I apply everything I have learned over the years? What does all of this look like? How can I help others? God, are you out there? I need help.

It took many years for me to process all of this and it took many failures before I was able to put it all together. The things that happened to me growing up were painful, leaving me to feel as though I was a failure. I didn't want to fail at this.

I remember reflecting, as I got older and into the work force, I had had my share of "meanie-pants" people. I had to work side-by-side with some of them. Some of them reminded me of being in grade school. These people were my supervisors, people I had to answer to, and some of them even wrote my paychecks. I had been surrounded by this my entire life. What could I do to change it?

Working with the hundreds of cancer kids that I met over the years brought clarity to me.

Let me tell you a story. I got an email one afternoon from a mommy whose son had been battling cancer for nearly a year. He had something called ALL, acute lymphoblastic leukemia. Many kids have to take steroids when they are battling cancer, and the steroids often make them gain weight. In Tommy's case, his nine-year-old little body had gained about forty pounds in a very short amount of time. The kids at school were calling him names and picking on him because of his weight gain. They didn't understand what cancer was. The students also did not understand that Tommy's weight gains were from the medicine.

I didn't know this family very well, and I wasn't very familiar with this type of cancer. The mom asked me if I would go to his school, be his "show and tell," and go to a few of his classes. Okay; she wanted me to go hang out with this young boy who is battling cancer and having a horrible time at school with his grades and his friends. My first thought was that I went through the same kind of thing for eight years. I was very familiar with this! What did she want me to "show?" My music! I can "tell" all about that! I can do this!

After clearing my visit with the school principal, we decided I would visit the school with Tommy and go to his reading class, lunch and music class. I showed up in that school with my sweet mohawk and everyone looked at me like I was a weirdo. I went to the office and the office lady looked at me like she was going to call the police. It is nauseating to me to see how people judge others. Anyway…I told her why I was there and asked her for her name. "My name is Mrs. Atz", she replied. I said, "It is a pleasure to meet you, ma'am; you have a beautiful school." I also wanted to tell her to stop being a meanie-pants, quit judging a book by its cover, and to wipe that judgmental look off her face, but I kept my thoughts to myself.

I met Tommy in his Reading class. When I walked in I said, "Hello, my name is Christopher Milo, and I'm here to visit with Tommy." You could have counted all the teeth in the room when I asked that question. Tommy jumped up from the circle he was sitting in and said, "Hi, Christopher Milo; thank you for coming to see me today!" He was all smiles! The kids all looked at him, thinking, "Who is this dude that just came in our class with the crazy hair?" It was so funny! I asked the teacher if I could read. I made funny voices and read much of the book wrong, but the kids almost peed their pants laughing so hard.

After I finished reading it was time for lunch. Thank God, because I was starving. I never left Tommy's side. I stood in the lunch line with him and sat with him while we ate our lunch. As you can imagine, I didn't blend in very well and I hardly fit in the little chairs at the lunch table. Every minute that went by, another student came over to us. They started giving Tommy high-fives and wanted to hang out with us. Everyone asked Tommy who his friend was. It was awesome to see the kids being cool to him. He felt safe and confident and had the sense of security that he had been missing. It was raining that day so all the kids went to their next period class early and had quiet time until the next period started.

As we proceeded to Tommy's music class, there was a line of kids following us around like a parade was in session. You could see the pride on Tommy's face. We made it to the music room and guess what I found? There was a grand piano in the music room! I told the teacher who I was and briefly why I was there. I asked if I could speak for a few minutes and the teacher said, "You can talk the entire period if you want! God bless you for coming to see him." Did a teacher just say "God bless you" in a public school? Sweet! I took over the class without the slightest clue of what I was doing! It was awesome!

I told the kids who I was and shared stories of what life on the road as a musician was like. I asked my friend Tommy to come up to the front of the class and the entire room clapped and stood up for him. He was fighting back tears. I could see in his face the same look I had on my face when I won the kickball game in the eighth grade. All of a sudden, he was important, he mattered, and he felt he had a purpose. It was the best!

I sat down on the piano bench and played my heart out for Tommy. The kids had never seen hands move as fast as mine. We wrote a song called "Tommy's Tune" and all the kids participated. We clapped. We sang. We danced. The students were hugging Tommy as I was leaving. I heard kids asking Tommy if they could be his friend. One boy asked Tommy if he wanted to have a playdate at his house over the weekend. It was beautiful and a Friday that I will remember forever.

About three hours later, I got a call from Tommy's mom. She could hardly talk on the phone because she was crying so hard from being so happy. Her little boy said he had the best day of his life and said that he had never had so many friends. When she picked him up from school, she saw all the kids hugging him, playing with him and including him. Tommy was a rock star and his mommy saw the Tommy she knew before cancer.

God knew what He was doing when He sent me to that school on that rainy Friday, because two days later, Tommy passed away.

I have dozens of stories just like Tommy's, but the same question remains. What am I supposed to do with all this information? It appears that I am being used for a mission or specific purpose. Is this my ministry? Is this my ultimate purpose? I believe that all to be true. I don't have the education or experience to be put in the hundreds of unique positions I have been in, but there is always a solution for me to give. Or is there? Do the real-world, real-life experiences I've had give me enough education to be able to help others?

I got on my knees one day, looked up to Heaven and said, *"I can't do this. I am not qualified to do this. I have a crazy haircut and the talents that I was blessed with. That's it. If I am going to continue doing this, I can't do it alone. God, I need you."*

I continue, to this day, going to schools with kids battling cancer and other illnesses. There is more to show and lots more to tell every year that God allows me to do the work that I do. I'm very thankful for the countless kids like me that have taught me so much throughout my life. They have helped me align myself and help me identify where the real needs are in communities all over the world. But how do I create something that will impact communities everywhere and be easy enough for everyone to understand?

I did. I created the "13 Messages from Milo" Professional Mentoring Program. It's simple! We build committees in schools and encourage everyone to work together. Students create goals and focus on one of the 13 Messages each week. Then repeat. Can it really be that simple? It is. There is a little more to it, but I'll show you when I come to your school.

I have learned that there are three key points in all of this:

1. Teachers, educators and the people who help raise our children on a daily basis.

2. The kids. Students of all ages from kindergarten to college.

3. The parents of the students, and anyone who has a child.

If all three of these key points are not on the same page, the school, the home and most certainly the community where all these people live, it will not be successful. You'll have disrespectful children, teachers who don't care, and parents who aren't engaged in what their kids are doing.

I want to tell you about an elementary school student for a moment. Let's say a second-grader. In most communities, to keep this generalized, the parent wakes up an hour before school, then wakes up the student, prepares and eats breakfast, puts the student on the bus or drives the student to school and then says "Tag, you're it," to the bus driver or the nice lady standing by the school door welcoming the kids. You've just given your child to someone else to safely and responsibly take care of your child before the tag returns to you. Then, "Tag," your student goes to class to meet the teacher, who you entrust to do the same thing. "Tag" again, when your bundle of joy gets to the lunch room and the three ladies standing there give your child food that will nourish their body and hold them over until they get to snack time or home. Then "Tag" one last time, as we repeat the beginning of the day, but now in reverse.

For every "Tag," there are staff members, as I refer to in key point number 1, people who take responsibility for your child. Parents expect today's educators to treat their children with dignity and respect, and in a safe environment: but do they know your family's core values? No! In the community that I live in, the entire world is represented. You'll find every race and religion, and somehow it seems to work, but is it really working?

If it's working, why do more schools each year request me at their schools? Why does the heroin epidemic gain momentum year after year? Why do most people first use drugs as teenagers? Why do millions of people start using drugs each year?

Why do we keep hearing stories about cutting and self-harm? Is your kid the bully at school? Who isn't teaching our children to say "No" to drugs and alcohol? Who is responsible for not loving your children enough that they feel the need to cut themselves for attention? Who is going to take responsibility?

I will, but I can't do it alone. Until we all work together and become aligned, nothing is going to change. Until we stop passing blame and pointing the finger at everyone else, nothing is going to change. Until we accept the fact that we all have to work hard and protect our children's eyes, ears and hearts from what they see, hear and worship, nothing is going to change. Aren't you tired of all the illness, hate, crime and anger? I am; that's why I turned to God.

I've heard every excuse in the book, from single parents, to family members getting shot and being on drugs, to "I just don't care." I hear "I just don't care" from parents, students and educators. My friends, we can't fix what happened yesterday. We can only move forward. Life might not have handed some of us golden tickets that would provide us all with not a care in the world, but, frankly, the Golden Ticket is out there. It is called the Bible.

Much like a puzzle, I have accumulated many of the pieces over the years. The pieces were from every emotion, every cut, every bruise, every fall and every ounce of pain that I felt from someone judging me, but every time I tried to put the puzzle together, it never fit right. When I tried to do things without His help, my flesh was not capable of obtaining the kind of results He desires. He wants us to seek Him first. As it says in Matthew 6:33, "Seek the Kingdom of God above all else, and live righteously, and he will give you everything you need."

I pray this for me and you, today and always. I struggle every day with one thing or another, but I can tell you this. My ultimate goal is to one day stand before God and say, "God, I don't have any talents left because I used everything you gave me." As far as I'm concerned, if I'm standing there saying that, I'm in the right place.

I think we are now figuring out the answer to the question at the beginning of this chapter. It doesn't really matter what I think. What He wants me to do with this information is to share it. Just like grade school, it took me a little longer than others to do certain things and this is no exception. Once I found Him and aligned myself right in His eyes, the rest fell into place. Why? Because it wasn't me trying to create a plan for me. It was me taking the time to listen and be obedient to what His plan is. This is a movement. Together, we can put this into motion and watch how God uses the "13 Messages from Milo" I'll say it again, it's not about me. Are you with me?

Christopher in the first grade trying to
figure out why

ten

The Professional Mentoring Program

"It is fascinating to me when He aligns things."
-Christopher Milo

A s I continued to process and pray, I had many influential people help me align this. I was all over the place with ideas. There was an endless amount of trial and error, but if I can make even a small positive impact on our youth today, I will continue dedicating my life to doing just that! Educators have often asked why students are so eager to listen to someone like me. It is actually pretty simple! I am not the parent and I am not the teacher. With my unique program and stories, students quickly and clearly see that I am someone who cares and understands what they are going through. I use real-life scenarios to drive the messages into the hearts and minds of people. I bring out the truth by telling the truth. The 13 Messages from Milo create a noninvasive environment that is welcoming to our youth, where walls come down and relationships are created. A small idea in a small group becomes a life-changing opportunity for an entire student body.

The "issues" started for me in about 4th grade. Common sense told me that was a good place to start. It worked! I learned that middle school was a perfect target for me to invest the program. Students are influential, transitioning, attentive and have a hunger for fitting in. Like me, students around grades four through six are trying to figure out who their friends are, where they fit in, who they should hang out with, and what is going on with all the personal changes in their lives. Without structure and simplicity, today's youth feel very lost, unmotivated and unloved. I have seen this last all the way through college. For those reasons and more, my program focuses on middle school to college. I quickly realized that there are three key points to making this successful. I could talk to students all day long, and I did, but I failed to think about the teachers who were with the students all day long. In addition to the teachers, who is the main source for leadership on a daily basis while these young learners are not in school? The parents.

When I started including the staff, students and parents in my program, it all made sense. There are national programs who have based their information on thirty years' worth of research. That doesn't work. I know this because I have been hired to present the program that was created thirty years ago. I have news for you: in our rapidly changing times, it is critical to stay with the current times and programming that can adapt to the needs of each individual school is mandatory.

Let me give you one example.

I went to two schools in the same town, twenty minutes from each other. It was like spending one day at a beach in sunny ninety-degree weather and one day on the cold ice in Alaska. One school had suicide issues where the other never had experienced suicide. One school had a heroin issue and the other did not. You would think the school that had the drug issue had the suicide issue, and in fact, that was not the case. If I went to every school and talked only about drugs and sex, it might scar the innocent minds of the students. I adapt my program to the needs of every school. That is why I need a minimum of four initial visits and that is why it works! In some cases, the leadership of the school is capable of continuing the program on their own. However, I've learned that the staff isn't the best choice to keep continued programming going. That is why I created the follow-ups "Phase I" and "Phase II." Today's teachers feel stretched, overworked and unappreciated. I see it firsthand. My goal is to keep children out of detention, encourage them to make better choices and goals, help them be on time, allow them to feel empowered and let them feel like they all matter. This will lower truancy issues, keep our young people out of juvenile court and one day, prevent them from spending the rest of their life in prison.

It excites me to see an idea ignite on a young face, not because my lesson was great, but because the student is smart and willing and made the effort to apply what they learned. I make sure the students know that they matter, they are loved, and they each have a purpose in life. Together, we work on figuring it all out! American homes implement the program, businesses embrace the program and its simplicity, and this is how my program is presented to schools.

What to expect when Christopher Milo comes to your school

DAY 1–The Staff Meeting–Assessment

During this time, Christopher will speak to teachers and explain what will happen during the time at your school. Through this introduction, Christopher will learn from the staff what they observe and their ideas on school opportunities. Depending on what information is shared, Christopher may find a need to discuss information with the school principal, guidance counselors and administration to better complete the assessment. Christopher will focus on a series of five fact-finding questions regarding the staff and students during the time together.

DAY 2–The Interruption Visit

With the help of the school principal and the understanding of the teachers, Christopher will tour the school to visit individual classrooms, and observe. These brief classroom visits will allow Christopher to ask questions and interact with students at their level. One of Christopher's favorite questions is "Now that we have known each other for a few minutes, tell me what I do for a living?" This question always produces some great answers such as, "You're a hair dresser—a shoe salesman—you ride a Harley—or you're a rock star!" We have found that students mimic their school behavior during these introductions by judging and creating opinions based on little to no information. Christopher encourages the students to ask more open-ended questions instead of jumping to conclusions. He then shares with the students what he really does and especially why he shaved his hair into a mohawk. Christopher's presence creates a high level of curiosity and desire to know more and when he informs the students that he is coming back for an all-school assembly, the excitement explodes. The teachers and administration may offer suggestions and areas of opportunity with individual students. This can enhance the time and program while Christopher is at your school.

DAY 3–The Assembly

Christopher returns for an in-school musical assembly. The student body has already visited with him while touring the school building and the excitement is exploding. During the assembly Christopher will introduce the student body to his "13 Messages from Milo" where they will understand how he uses his talents. Between his story of being paralyzed over twenty years ago and being told he would never walk again, and his incredible piano skills, it will be an assembly that will be talked about the entire school year. It typically lasts an hour. Christopher brings his own digital piano, sound system, and banners, one reading "13 Messages from Milo" and one reading "Motivate, Encourage and Empower."

DAY 4–Parent Meeting

In order to cultivate a positive climate and culture in a school, three areas of focus are required: school staff, the student body, and parents. Christopher's unique approach includes a specialized meeting with parents. During this meeting, he presents an overview of what has transpired over the last several days. Christopher highlights all the things he has learned during his time at the school and exactly what the parents can do to help with the growth and development of their children and community. This meeting continues to be the most effective of the 13 Messages from Milo program. As always, students are welcome to attend this meeting!

This entire program is executed with teacher and principal awareness. In order for Christopher to be effective in your school, he will need the help of the teachers, the administration, the lunch ladies, and the guidance counselors, as well as parent feedback. With this interaction, Christopher is able to give personalized examples of bullying, self-harm, and drug or alcohol issues that might have taken place in your school or the community. Every school is different, and each has their own concerns to be addressed. This is why the program is customized to fit uniquely to your school. The more information that is shared, the better the program will be. The "13 Messages from Milo" Professional Mentoring Program is proven to enhance your school in many ways, including:

- Positively impacts the entire school, including the school body, teachers and the administration
- Cultivates a school atmosphere where students are eager to learn and attend classes
- Excites the student body by giving them purpose, which creates hope and a "can-do" attitude
- Kindness becomes exceptional and inappropriate becomes appropriate

Congratulations, your search is over once you choose the "13 Messages from Milo" Professional Mentoring Program!

eleven

A Parent, Student And Teacher...
With My Reply

If you do not have the basics in your life, keep trying, keep

searching and don't give up.

-Christopher Milo

I've included real-life scenarios in this chapter. I've included them in this book because of the value it can have. When I teach my "13 Messages from Milo" Professional Mentoring Program in schools, I'll often meet with the parents of the students during my fourth visit. I've learned that if one parent has a question, it is not uncommon for other parents to want to discuss the same or similar issues. I've also learned that many parents lack the courage to ask questions. This can happen for many reasons, including the embarrassment of having a child going through the situation, or the feeling that no one is going to understand if they speak up.

I get hundreds of emails with questions and thoughts from parents every year. Some of these emails are included in this chapter.

This first email I would like to share is from a mother in Kentucky who had a situation with her eighth-grade son being treated differently by a teacher. As with any issues, I personally review all the documentation as well as behavioral plans from the school regarding each situation. I have kept the emails the way I received them. Her email reads:

Christopher,

Here is some additional information that you requested. It will probably be pretty lengthy because I'm going to write it for myself as well.

Slater just turned 14, is in 8th grade and very popular. A bright boy that teachers tell me is finished with his work in 10 minutes while others are struggling, could be a great leader if he applied himself, that everyone watches him and likes him. He is very athletic and plays football, soccer and wrestles for the middle school. Slater is a typical teenager and will test you. Especially if you are not a good teacher! For some reason this is a requirement of his! He loves to be the center of attention and make people laugh even at his own expense.

It basically started with a new teacher that Slater started having issues with. I sent my husband to meet her at Open House. The first thing she said to him was, "I think your son has an issue with me because I'm a young female." Whoa!!! What??? She knew him for 15 days! How could she make that assumption and tell his father? I found out she was treating him differently than the other children. (Ex: another child (teacher's son) sat in an unassigned seat for the entire day. The next day he did the same, so Slater moved. She immediately screamed at Slater to go back to his seat. Then she looked at the other child and told him to move back as well. A couple of weeks later I found all the kids were going to have to take an additional Math class. I emailed to find out who he was going to have because we were already having problems with his current teacher.

Note: As you continue reading, you will see information suggesting multiple correspondences that were forwarded to me for my review. For privacy reasons, I did not include them.

The 3rd correspondence was generated by the Algebra teacher (this is the first correspondence that was generated by a teacher and at the end she tells me she will let me know at the end of the week how he is doing. I have not received a response *to date) and I found out it was a generic email that went to several parents but changed the students name. So obviously he is not acting alone.*

Attached are a couple of the write-ups which he served detention for and lost the ability to wrestle for a week. On one they led me to believe he was harassing another child about being gay. It was actually one of his good friends that was bear hugging another friend and he responded with what is on the write-up. Each time he would receive a write up we would discuss his behavior and disruptions with him. Then we would take his phone or give other punishment to him. It wasn't until the write-up on 12/3 that everything went crazy...

The kids have between 3 and 4 minutes to change classes. They are not allowed to carry their backpacks with them (it is a tripping hazard for the teachers in the classroom) so they have to go to their lockers in between each class and get their information for the next one. They also can't have more than two tardies in a 4.5-week period or they receive some type of punishment for that. They got out of 5th period late and he went to Algebra class (last class in the day) and sometime during class he had to go to the restroom. He asked if he could go and she yelled at him and told him "No, you may not go!" Another student that sits beside him said I guess you'll have to go here.

He unbuttoned the button on his jeans, he said, to prevent his jeans from pressing on his bladder. The teacher sent him to the hall while she tried to get someone from the office to come and get him. She finally sent another child to the office to bring the Asst. Principal back to get him. He went to the office with him and was there until after school. NEVER being allowed to go to the restroom! 4 weeks prior to that he separated his ribs and bruised his kidney in wrestling and they aren't allowing my child to use the restroom!! The Asst. Principal did not call me that day but Slater told me after practice what happened. When I did get the call the next day, Wednesday at 3:45 in the afternoon, he informed me that Slater would have an in-school suspension, he would not be allowed to go on the field trip on the 20th of Dec. and he was not allowed to go to KYA the next day. All for this one incident! I was mad! Heck no, the child shouldn't have done what he did, but isn't this overkill?

KYA is Kentucky Youth Assembly, a program that the kids had stayed after school once a week for a couple months to prepare. Description – it's a three-day experimental learning conference in which students participate directly in a simulation of the Commonwealth's democratic process. Acting as Senators and Representatives, students write, debate, and vote on legislation that affects them... Their conference was scheduled for Thursday, Friday and Saturday in Louisville and they traveled to Frankfort to the General Assembly to present their projects on Friday. They were required to wear suits, ties and dress shoes. The cost to go was $230 and he was all packed *for it. Like I said on Wednesday at 3:45, the day before they were leaving for the trip, is when I was notified. They didn't even tell him.*

Thursday – Don and I went to the school in the morning to meet with the Principal about the matter. Slater went to morning assembly before going to the office to serve his in-school suspension. Two students came up to him and told him that his Social Studies teacher discussed his situation with one of her classes and said that he did not receive enough punishment, he should have been suspended. I would have to think the school prohibits this type of discussion of a pupil. Our meeting did not go well. Still at this point, I have not received the write-up from the teacher. The Asst. Principal told me that the teacher was in the middle of instruction when he interrupted to go to the restroom and that she was going to let him go after she was finished (she made no mention of that to him in class). Slater told me they were working on a work sheet at the time. I asked the Principal why Slater was not allowed to go the restroom. I said, "I could see if he did it habitually but he has only gone twice in her room." He said it was his understanding that he asks 3 to 4 times a day in her class! Oh please!! Do you think a teacher would allow this to go on every day? Heck no! This would have given them more excuse to write him up. I can't believe anything that comes out of their mouths. He then told me that they were completing a worksheet and she instructed them to get out their notebooks when this happened. I told him that is probably why he asked to go then because he didn't think he would have another chance. He said, "But that is the most critical time to be in class." Really??? He wasn't there the rest of class or the next day and every time he gets a write-up the Asst. Principal pulls him out of the same class. He is still maintaining an "A" though. Then he tells me that Slater unbuttoned his pants and started to pulled his fly down! What??? Where did this come from???? There was no mention of that on Wednesday when the Asst. Principal talked to me. He told me that he wasn't allowed to go to KYA because they couldn't trust him. I told him to ask the KYA teacher that has been spending time with Slater what she thinks. He said he already did and she said, "Slater has not attended regularly and he does not work as hard as some of the other students." Not attended regularly? Then where has he been? SEE KYA.docx

He served his time on Thursday at school and I made him go to wrestling practice. He said he would go but he wasn't going to do anything. When I went to pick him up I talked to the coach. I asked him, "How did today go?" He said, "He came in thinking that he wasn't going to do anything. I could tell this has been hard on him. I told him to get his shorts and shoes on and go out there and take it out on somebody." He did and was practicing when I got there. Coach told me he was contacted and strongly encouraged to go hard on him. He

105

said, *"I'm not jumping on that band wagon. I know the kid is having a hard time and if I thought it would help, I would go and talk to them."* *Coach isn't a school employee, he owns a bakery and for him to be contacted it had to have been on purpose. They just don't pass each other in the hall. Friday morning, he started having panic attacks. I took him to school to be with the teacher that talks about him in front of others, the one that says he isn't showing up to class or participating, the one that treats him differently than every other student, the Asst. Principal that stands and stares at him all through lunch and I left him. I stayed home from work that day in case he needed me. I told him to text me and let me know if it goes away. It wasn't going away so I called his doctor. I explained the situation to him and asked what I should do. He told me to go and get him, remove him from the situation. The weather was getting bad and the school decided to release early so I waited until then to pick him up.*

My husband, Don, called to talk to the Superintendent but he was out so the secretary directed him to the Asst. Superintendent. That conversation was pointless. He said it sounds like Slater needs to go on a program. He wanted Don to find out from the coach who told him to go hard on Slater and told Don to confront the teacher that talked about him in front of her class. Really??? Do these people not work for him??? What kind of a show are they running? The superintendent never called us back.

On Wednesday, the same day the Asst. Principal called me, I got an email from one of his teachers with others carbon copied. All of them wanted to sit down with Don and I. SEE Meeting. docx. We met the next Tuesday, Dec 10th. At first it was five of his teachers and Don and I. Then the Asst. Principal and Principal joined us. They proposed a Behavior Plan for him. SEE Behavior Plan.pdf. In short, he must maintain 18 out 20 "Y's" in each class in order to not receive punishment (this is listed on page two) he is supposed to have a reward for the weeks he maintains 90% or above but we have yet to see this in the three weeks he has maintained above 90%. The Behavior Plan is supposed to be texted to me at the end of each day. We agreed to this Behavior Plan and assumed this started a new slate and he would be punished according to this plan. But they always change the rules.

I received a call in the afternoon of Jan. 8th, the day the kids went back to school after winter break. It was the Asst. Principal letting me know that Slater had been written up on Dec. 19th! SEE Dec 19 Writeup.pdf and email correspondence SEE Correspondence for Write up Dec 19.docx. As you can see, I was not happy about the teacher allowing the behavior to continue. This was not how Don and I viewed the agreement as it was presented to us. This Behavior Plan was designed to provide me with information daily about his behavior since I was not receiving any before this. Slater said he had no idea the write-up was coming. He said she was cutting up with them and didn't seem upset. Anyway, the correspondence sums it up. The reply I got did not address the majority of questions I asked and his punishment was not given according to the Behavior Plan. He had to serve a break detention, was not permitted to wrestle with the team at a match and had to serve a 3-hour detention after school. Again, 3 punishments were given to him.

On Monday the 13th he started a new class for the new 9-week period. The teacher gave him a "N" and commented "using chat, not the only one", Chat is like messaging on the computers. Another child sent a "chat" to Slater and he responded "hey". He was made to stand in the hall for 15 minutes while the other child received no punishment. The Asst. Principal told Don it was because he was on a point system and the other child was not. I thought the "N" on the paper was sufficient. We were lead to believe that maintaining a 90% on the sheet was the goal but they are still assigning punishments for him while maintaining that.

Yesterday he received a "N" in a class for wrestling with another child. When I got to wrestling practice to pick him up, one of his friends came up to me and apologized for getting him in trouble. He told me it was all his fault. The other child approached him from behind at the end of class and put him in a half nelson. He was not the one wrestling but again the one to receive a mark for doing so. At least she didn't punish as well.

I am going to call the Superintendent to schedule a meeting but really do not have high hopes of achieving anything. We have pretty much exhausted every avenue at this point and do not see any other way to protect him but to seek legal counsel. Slater does not have any issues with other kids, only teachers and administration. Daily he sees himself being treated differently and being punished excessively for the same things other students are doing. We worry that this will carry on to high school and that he won't have a chance to be a normal kid but will be labeled from the start. Ex: he started gym class on Monday for the new 9 weeks and the teacher told them there was no food, drink, or gum allowed in the gym. He asked why they shouldn't allow gum and the kids started to answer his question. Slater said that kids could blow bubbles and the teacher replied, "Slater, am I going to have to hurt you on the first day?" Slater said, "I only meant that it could be a distraction to other kids." The teacher responded, "Like you're being right now?"

I know I have bombarded you with information but it was therapeutic for me to get it out. I'm not sure what you could do for this situation. If you have any advice, please let me know.

God bless you and thanks so much for trying to help.

Holy cats! Let me begin by saying this. I hope and pray every kid in the world has a parent like Slater does. It's obvious to me where the issues are. Let's pull out some important key points:

- The parents never gave up during this situation. Believe in your kids! If you know you are raising your children to be responsible and respectful, don't give up on them! Take the time they deserve to be parents like this mom did.

- If you ever hear that your child, or any child, is having his or her dirty laundry being shared in class, handle it immediately. Often I hear parents say, "It's not about my child so I stay out of it." Here's a news flash: it could be! If parents would stand together and address the needs of our kids, I promise you things would be better. I am by no means suggesting that you put your nose in everyone's business. I am suggesting you pay attention and **listen** to your children and their friends. Years ago, I heard someone say, "It takes a village to raise a child." They're right.

- In this case, the parents always showed Slater love. Love was in the form of not giving up on him, taking away a device and correcting him when it was needed, and so on. Love is the key to success, and it looks like many things depending on your situation.

I've met over 100,000 students in my career. I've spoken to each one face-to-face. I've met thousands of teachers in various schools, and it isn't uncommon to see one teacher who will stand out. This was a clear case of a teacher and Leadership team who had a set of their own issues and took it out on a student. Do you know how I know this? I do my best to stay in touch with the moms and dads who reach out to me. After two years of trying to figure out a solution to this mom's concern, this is what I found out.

Christopher!!! So glad to hear from you. I'm thankful that we only had 4 months left to get through our middle school year fiasco and that the person the superintendent put in charge of our case was Slaters elementary school principal. He knew Slater and could see that the treatment he was receiving was not warranted. He talked to the teachers and assured us we would have no further problems through the end of the school year. We obviously still have communication with the principal since Sally is in middle school and Slater wrestles with his son on the high school team.

Slater has been doing great in high school. The only teachers he has had any issues with are the football coaches... they are mad at him for quitting football. Treatment over his weight was becoming a big issue. The coaches were constantly on him about gaining weight and this was everyday…at school, on the track field, at church and even working Bingo which was required of us to be on the team. I heard it all the time so I know it was happening to him at school when I wasn't there. Things like– Slater go get another burger, Slater how much do you weigh? Slater my daughter is bigger than you and she's 7! I know I was tired of hearing it and he was so stressed out over it that he finally had to make a choice. He told them he was taking his talents elsewhere! Funny kid…but he did just that. As a sophomore he went to state in wrestling (126 lbs.) and is currently ranked 15th in the state, in track he placed 7th in state in the 4x800 and in soccer they won district. He continues with a 4.0 GPA and is still on the National Honor Society and in Gifted and Talented for Art. Recently he has been selected to participate in a Youth Leadership program within the community. It was established by the Chamber of Commerce in 1996. It lasts 6 months and starts in September.

This summer (2016) he has been attending wrestling and soccer camps and practicing his driving. He can obtain his license in July.

God bless you and your beautiful family

The Kentucky mom.

It is such an awesome feeling when I hear good results. This family:

- **LISTENED** to each other
- Was **CURIOUS** and did not stop until the results changed
- Understood the importance of **COMMUNICATION** and knew how to communicate
- Maintained a **POSITIVE** attitude
- **TRUSTED** each other
- **WORKED TOGETHER** to uncover the truth
- Was **GENUINE** in their approach and did not set out to harm anyone—They only wanted what was best for their son
- Had to **BE CREATIVE**: There was a need for change. Not knowing what that change was, they still embraced it.
- **USED THEIR TALENTS** and resources instead of giving up or giving in.
- Had to **COACH** their son at times. They never failed to stand up for their son, which is an **INSPIRATION** to any child. They **ACCEPTED** change and **USED THEIR TALENTS** to come up with realistic solutions to their concerns.

This is an A+ in my grade book! It is clear to me that when God is in control of things, the outcome is good. We must remember that things do not happen in our time, but in His time. Slater, wherever you are, I trust you are doing what you do best, being you! I'm proud of you, buddy!

Not all of the emails I receive are an inspiring flowing river of happiness. Some are very hurtful and hard for even me to read. As a father, I would be devastated with this next situation. This is from a troubled teen who I met at her school.

So I grew up with an alcoholic and an abusive father and dealt with that for the first 13 years of my life. Around there I met this kid that was cooler than me and at age 13, I thought I "loved" this kid like any teenage girl. He got me into the church and I became best friends with his mother who was my church group leader. His family was there for me through it all. When my grandfather passed away, and when child services came which were the 2 huge factors. At this point my life had been pretty normal. My dad continued to drink but stopped being abusive. And the kid I "loved" had broken up with me and gotten back together with me for almost a year until he started smoking he pulling away from the church while I was still going. After he started smoking and doing drugs all of his morals had changed and mine stayed the same. We were at a retreat away from home and he told me that if I didn't start giving him what he "wanted" that he was going to cheat on me or whatever. He continued to say not only this but things like "you're a sl**" "you're disgusting" "you should just kill yourself" until I caved because

I felt so poorly of myself. With that he would also punch me because he thought it was "funny" or whip me with this towel until I bled, or choked me to see how long I could hold my breath. I never told anyone what I did with him or what he had done to me. At this point I'm a freshman when he started hitting me and using me. I didn't want anyone else calling me a sl** or calling me weak for letting him hit me. People called me his dog. And he'd agree and laugh. I ended up one day being "late". I told him and he told me that it wasn't him that I was a sl**, etc. I didn't tell anyone except my sister, and somehow the whole school found out the next day. It was also the last day of school anyways. My sister had told my mom and my mom told me that I had a choice and that I had to think about them. I already knew what my choice was but somehow my mom kept going against me when she told me she'd support me. The guy had told me to get rid of it or raise a child on my own. My mom took me to this place and told me it was just a check-up. I walk in and they start giving me all these alternatives. My mom looked at me and told me I had no choice and that she didn't want me going through with what I believed was right. After everything was over from that "check up" I cried and cried and cried. A week later the head leader messages me saying I am not "spiritual" enough to give students guidance (I was a leader my freshman year) that I was a sinner, as if my sins were worse than others. He told me that I could never talk to my youth group girls ever again *never give them advice or make sure they are okay because I'm not "capable" of doing so. He asked me to not return to the church and that he hopes I find the right path again. When he kicked me out and kept the guy there that triggered everything and pulled me out of my shock of everything. That night I got the message…. was when I started cutting. It was summer and I never left my bed. NEVER. Not even to eat. I couldn't eat. I couldn't sleep. I couldn't stop crying. My mom never noticed how depressed I was until I broke down and told her I wanted to kill myself I wanted to die. And that I tried. What's worse is that I get punished for saying things like that! My phone got taken away and I got put on anti-depressants. School had started and I have been on the anti-depressants for about 3 weeks. And people started asking me questions and I'd lie to them. I found out it was the guy telling everyone that I was a killer and a murder (I never told him. My mother said I had a miscarriage) kids followed me around asking me if I needed them to push me down the stairs, or if I used a rusty hanger, kids told me to kill myself, I've heard it all. Kids still follow me around screaming "abortion" because that's a "trigger" word my counselor called it. It makes me cringe every time I think of it. When all that was going on, the guy was talking to a girl and she wanted to know if what he did to me was true, I told her it was true sparing some details and only telling her to be careful. She told the whole school some of the things he had done to me and the next day he calls me threatening to kill me telling me to kill myself or he'll do it for me that I'm worthless and that any guy who dated me would have done the same thing except worse. His friends harassed me calling me names a liar and what not. I got tripped down the stairs on multiple occasions, I tried pretending to "sleep in" to avoid going to school but my mom sent me anyways and my teacher saw the cuts on my arms and pulled me into the hallway to talk to me. I cried and told her everything because like I said in the earlier messages, I never actually had someone to talk to that truly cared. This all went on for the rest of my sophomore year. That summer I ended up hanging out with an old friend that I haven't seen in a while and I talked to him about everything and I thought I could trust him with it. He asked if we could go watch a movie at his house. I thought that was fine. No one was there except for him and me. We start watching the movie and he starts to touch me and I told him to stop and he continued. He raped me... And then took me home. Never told anyone never let it show nothing. One of my other exes found out that me and this kid hung out and demanded I tell him what happened because he "already knew" and wanted to hear it from me. I told him thinking he would understand and he told the whole lunch room and everyone again, told me I was lying, why would I lie, that guy would never do that, he's not that type of person, go kill yourself, you're only good for sex anyways, that's all you are worth, etc. At this point in time*

I started failing my chemistry bc I was also being harassed by my teacher for other reasons (doesn't work at school anymore) and I just kind of gave up on myself and my life. I dropped out and went online. Where I had no issues, I was safe, and away from the hurt. Even though I was/am still hurting. I came back this year hoping that I can push myself and ignore the comments, confront the people spreading rumors and in the process help others. Which honestly I think is working out pretty well. I am still battling with self-harm and depression. No matter how hard I try nothing can make the thoughts of my past go away. It's hard to think positively of yourself when every day for 3-4 years you've had not only one, but a bunch of people tell you how worthless you are, that you're a sl**, a murderer, waste of space, that I should have died when I tried to kill myself and it didn't work, that I should cut a little deeper, that I never deserve to be happy. When you are told that every day, it's hard not to believe it. I fight those internal comments now or at least I try. I want to be the person that someone can say "yeah! I had someone there for me" because I never truly had someone to trust and I want kids like me to know that they do.

Let's review. Beyond lacking leadership, this young teen had:
- A father who did not show **LOVE**
- A mother who could not **ACCEPT** the fact that a choice was made by this teen

118

- No students and family supporting her; they only hurt her in one way or another for **BEING CURIOUS**
- No one to **INSPIRE** her enough to lead her down a path that was not destructive
- No **COACH** that she could trust
- No leadership around her **BEING GENUINE**
- No parents who **WORK TOGETHER** like this scenario
- No mother who trusted in God. She chose to **BE CREATIVE** without His help
- Nobody that recited Proverbs 3:5-6, "**TRUST** in the Lord with all your heart and lean not on your own understanding. Acknowledge Him in all your ways and He shall direct your path."
- No responsible leader to **COMMUNICATE** with
- No people around her who would **LISTEN** in a non-judgmental way
- No leadership around her **BEING POSITIVE**
- No people encouraging her to **USE YOUR TALENTS**, yet they discouraged her for her choices

I hope and pray that after reading these two examples it is very clear why I teach the "13 Messages from Milo." If you don't have the basics in your life, keep trying, keep searching, and don't give up. You can see in the first example that when a scenario has all of the "13 Messages from Milo" being practiced, the results are wonderful. You can also see in the second scenario that when the "13 Messages from Milo" aren't being practiced, the results can be chaotic.

It sounds pretty simple, right? Not always. I'm always learning and growing, and recently learned in my walk about generational curses. Have you ever looked at yourself in the mirror and asked yourself, "How did I get this nose"? Have you ever seen yourself in a video clip and said to yourself, "I sound just like my mother!"

I am certain your mother is lovely. However, if your mom, dad, grandmother or grandfather have any of what I like to call "yesterday's yuck," there's a very good possibility that you have it too! These are called generational curses and are talked about throughout the Bible. I would like to share two examples in an effort to assist with this explanation.

> *The Lord is long-suffering and slow to anger, and abundant in mercy and lovingkindness, forgiving iniquity and transgression; but He will by no means clear the guilty, visiting the iniquity of the fathers upon the children, upon the third and fourth generation.*
> *—Numbers 14:18 AMP*

Keeping mercy and lovingkindness for thousands, forgiving iniquity and transgression and sin, but Who will by no means clear the guilty, visiting the iniquity of the fathers upon the children and the children's children, to the third and fourth generation.
　　　　　　　　　　　　　　　　　— Exodus 34:7 AMP

The next steps to all of this are to repent and forgive.

Step 1:　　　Repent

verb

feel or express sincere regret or remorse about one's wrong-doing or sin.

"the priest urged his listeners to repent"

synonyms: feel remorse, regret, be sorry, rue, reproach oneself,
　　　　　　be ashamed, feel contrite; be penitent, be remorseful,
　　　　　　be repentant "the senator claims to have repented"

view or think of (an action or omission) with deep regret or remorse.

"Marian came to repent her hasty judgment."

archaic

feel regret or penitence about.

"I repent me of all I did."

Step 2:   Forgive

for·give

fər'giv/

verb

1. stop feeling angry or resentful toward (someone) for an offense, flaw, or mistake.

   "I don't think I'll ever **forgive** David **for** the way he treated her"

   synonyms: pardon, excuse, exonerate, absolve; More

   o   stop feeling angry or resentful toward someone for (an offense, flaw, or mistake).

   "they are not going to pat my head and say **all is forgiven**"

As a Christian, you accept Jesus Christ as your Lord and Savior. After that, simply follow steps 1 and 2. You can feel confident that awesome change is soon to come!

Before we move on, I want to share one more story that will be a blessing to you because it certainly is for me. What is most unique about this story, is that a dear friend of mine, Chris K., told me a similar story that had taken place several years ago. I feel like he told me his story to help me prepare for what I was going to encounter.

I received a contract to work with a new middle school. As with all of my programs, my first visit is always with the staff. We review a series of five questions and discuss what they can expect during my next three visits. I often do a Q&A at the end of my meeting so everyone can better understand the needs of the school.

During a recent visit, a young teacher who had been teaching for only two years shared with me that she had several students to whom I should pay special attention. It's not uncommon for teachers to have particular students that may need more attention during my visits. Anna was a big problem. The teacher told me that Anna constantly sleeps in class, which was causing her grades to suffer. When I asked the teacher why she thought Anna was doing so bad in her fifth-grade class, the teacher said this to me.

"I haven't been able to put my finger on it. She is often late for first period, she puts her books away, and she's rarely prepared for class." I asked, "Did you ask her what was wrong?" She said, "Yes, and she said she was tired. But Mr. Milo, this is what is most frustrating for me. If I'm going to have my lesson plans prepared on time and all of my testing organized, the least she could do is show up to class prepared and ready to go. Some of these kids just don't get it." She went on, "I have to pick up both a three-year-old and a five-year-old from daycare every day, and then go home and prepare dinner. My husband and

I both work full time and I still have to do all the ironing and laundry…" On…and on…and on, all about herself!

The issue is with the fifth-grade little girl, not with her. I thought, "If you're going to get a degree in education and sign up to be a teacher, you must realize that being a teacher comes with many hats!" But as I normally do, I continued to stay quiet, respectful and attentive.

As I prepared to leave, I told Anna's teacher that I would pay attention to Anna when I came back to the school in a few days and proceeded to head out the door. "Oh my goodness!" I just shook my head and prayed for both Anna and the teacher.

I showed up early for school a few days later. I immediately found Mrs. Meanie Pants and her fifth-grade class. In an uplifting tone of voice, and with a huge smile, I said, "Well good morning, Mrs. Teacher!" She replied, "Class, this is Mr. Milo and he will be joining us today for class. Mr. Milo, would you like to speak to the class?" With the same energy I replied, "Heavens, no; I think I'll just observe for now!"

It was easy to spot Anna. First chair, second row from the door with her head down the moment the teacher began class. I typically address the class but this time I grabbed my bag and invited three kids out in the hallway to chat: two complete strangers and Anna. I made sure Anna was last. I asked the students a few quick questions and left each of them with an inspiring thing to think about. I said to Anna that I noticed she had her head down on her desk. She said she was tired. I told her I was tired too, and that I hadn't wanted to get out of bed that day. I asked her a few more questions and asked her if she would feel better if she went to the nurse's office. She smiled and said yes! She looked exhausted. She looked as though she had not eaten well, and her energy level was zero. I told her I would get her books and to go to the office to put her head down.

When I went back into the classroom without Anna, I knew at that moment that I hadn't made the teacher's Christmas card list. She was so upset that I had dismissed her and given in to a 5th grader. Needless to say, my day was very long in this school.

I left the school about 7:45 p.m. On my way back to the hotel, I drove around the neighborhood where my hotel was so I could clear my head and enjoy some fresh air. While the sun was preparing to rest for the day, I slowed down because I saw four people on the side of the road walking. As I got closer I noticed they weren't walking but were working. I recognized Anna and she was with her little brother, mom and dad. It was clear they were picking up cans for recycling and I pulled over and shined my headlights in the grassy area where they were looking for cans. I got out of my truck and said to her father, "May I help?" He said, "That would be great; who are you?" I greeted Anna by name and introduced myself to the family. I told them I met Anna at school that day and had nothing to do that evening. I worked until about 9:30 p.m. with Anna and her family. I thanked Anna's father for allowing me to help. I gave Anna and her little brother high-fives and wished the mom a blessed evening. Her family was awesome. It was obvious to me that there were some financial issues, which became clearer when her daddy told me he had lost his job a few months before. They were the sweetest family. I was exhausted! I couldn't imagine how this family must feel.

This explained just about everything! I couldn't wait to get to school the next day. How was I going to respect this situation? How was I going to guard the dignity of these kind people? It was really hard to sleep that night knowing that I was in a beautiful hotel room with room service and my every need being met, while this family was in such rough shape.

That next morning, I got to school about thirty minutes early. I spoke to the principal and shared my previous evening with her. When she got done wiping the tears from her eyes, she told me that she had had no idea the family was going through this, and that it was no wonder Anna was having these difficulties. Anna was tired, hungry and certainly embarrassed. If I were Anna, I would have felt the same.

Guess what I did? I had one of the kids working in the office go to Anna's classroom and say that she was needed in the office. I wasn't going! Are you kidding me? I needed to stay far away from Mrs. Meanie Pants until I took care of Anna. I had asked the man working at the breakfast buffet at my hotel to make me 4 to-go boxes of food. I told him to smash as much food in those containers as he could fit. I told him I get real hungry throughout the day. He never said a word to me, but put plastic wrap around each of them. They were so heavy!

I ran out to my truck and got the food while Anna was on her way to the office. The principal and I took Anna into the conference room with one container of food and I told her I wanted her to eat. When she opened that white foam container, she looked like she had just won an all-expenses-paid trip around the world that would last forever! You know what that little girl said to me? "Mr. Milo, I'm really not hungry; could I take this home instead? All she wanted to do was make sure her family was fed. I showed her the three other containers of food, and you should have seen her eat! And eat and cry and then eat some more. Within minutes, she told the principal all about her evening. You couldn't slow her down, she was so pumped up. It was like a different kid! The principal told Anna to go to the nurse's office to rest. She smiled and took a nap. I went from being emotional to feeling like a raging bull stuck in a cage. Yes, I was on my way to visit Anna's teacher. The principal asked me if she could go. I said no.

This time, I pulled the teacher out of class. The principal arranged for someone to cover her next class. It took everything in my power to keep calm. I was very kind. After I explained to the teacher what I had just been through with Anna, she felt horrible. She apologized to me for her selfish behavior and asked what she needed to change and move forward.

This was the attitude I wanted to see from the beginning! I have met some of the finest people our educational system has to offer. I feel confident that Anna's teacher will grow to be one of them. It is always important to get to know your students. The biggest takeaway for me in all of this is to listen first and then engage. Anna's teacher wanted to talk first and then listen. She was overcome with pride and more concerned about herself.

Let's discuss pride for just a moment. Anna was obviously too proud to share her family's failures. Mrs. Teacher was too proud to engage with Anna, which resulted in feelings of disrespect and anger and neither party got any help. Where is the good in any of that? There is none.

I'm convinced that I was placed in that school, with hundreds of students at that time and place, just to meet Anna. About a week later I sent my weekly follow-up e-mail to the principal to see how things were going with my "13 Messages from Milo" program. She told me it was going great and was eager to quickly change the subject. She told me that the day I had been at the school, she delivered the three remaining meals to Anna's family. The very next day, Anna's dad told the principal that while they were eating the food, he got a call from his old boss. His company had had to shut their doors for five months due to their lack of contracts. However, they got a huge contract for three years, which not only made room for his job but for another twelve men!

In all of these scenarios, what I want you to take away is this. As parents, we have to be the example in all we do. I'm far from being a perfect parent, but I can tell you this. I strive every day to be an encouragement to everyone God puts before me. I do this by practicing the "13 Messages from Milo." I do this by offering empathy and sympathy, and by putting others feelings before mine. None of this is about you. None of this is about me. What can you do for someone else today? How can you be a blessing to someone else? Write your ideas down if you need to. Write down the names of people you want to help in some way. Then, write down a plan of how you plan to help.

_____

_____

_____

_____

_____

_____

_____

_____

_____

_____

_____

<u>twelve</u>

<u>It's Not About Me</u>

It's not about me. It's about you and what you can do for Him.
-Christopher Milo

After performing countless assemblies, shows, music performances and keynote speaking engagements, people of every age ask me the same question.

Are you a Christian?

Do you think it's because I wear cool shoes? Is it because I wear a cross around my neck? Is it because I sometimes wear a Mohawk? Is it because I have a wonderful talent and have chosen to not live in pride? Why is this one of the top three questions I get asked? The public school system doesn't permit me to openly discuss being a Christian or even discuss any religion while on the school property. I always follow the rules that are put in place by the educational system, but I still get that question. It proves to me that when you're craving the love and understanding of God and what he has done for us, the Holy Spirit shines God's glory right through us and our actions. Your actions speak so loudly I can hardly hear a word you say. It's never natural, because it's supernatural.

The true tragedy is that every time I am asked that question, society has forced me to keep my thoughts and feelings quiet and to myself. What a tragedy.

If you are interested in becoming a Christian, you can contact me through www.christophermilo.com and I will make sure to share the next steps with you on how to do that. I never discuss religion in schools, yet your kids are asking me about Jesus and any help you can give is going to help everyone in the long run.

For those Christian parents who are interested in giving your children the best gift you could ever give them, please follow these instructions:

Step 1.   Pray and bring your children into the Father's courtroom.

Step 2.   Repent for your children: any failures, lies of the enemy, anything.

(Intercessors do for others what they can't do for themselves, until they can. Take authority (you need it) the mother, father, etc...)

Step 3.   Parents need to repent for the things they have said about their child, like "I don't understand why my child has (fill in the blank)."

The accuser, Satan, is using the words of the parents against the children in the courtroom which gives him the legal right to affect the child's destiny.

Step 4.   Speak and prophesy your child's destiny. Speak it into existence! "He/she will be healthy, will be successful, will be happy, will be able to work through any issue, will win souls, et cetera..."

Step 5.   Rebuke the Spirit of Depression or the negative in the child's life.

At this point you can righteously and legally attack the devil!

Step 6.   Now say, "Satan, I rebuke you! According to Ephesians 5:14, "Therefore He says: "Awake, you who sleep, arise from the dead, and Christ will give you light." Leave my child alone **now,** in Jesus' name. Amen."

Step 7. Pray this:

Prayer

God, we want to thank you. You are our Father, you are our friend and also our judge. We want to come before the courts of heaven by faith and we want to ask You, Lord, that verdicts will be rendered in our favor. You created each person in the book with a destiny from heaven. Lord, I want to ask that every legal issue that is being used against any person, any family line... Lord, that legal issue will be broken and removed.

Lord, in Jesus' name, I repent, for any sin, transgression, or iniquity. I claim Col 2:14, anything against me, any accusation, anything that is contrary to me, I remove, and nail it to your cross. Lord any accusation is removed by the blood of Jesus and Lord, and we grant you, as judge, the legal right to render a verdict so that I can have the destiny that was written in the Lamb's Book of Life about me.

In Jesus' name, Amen.

I am combining talents, gifts, and abilities, and at the end of the day, none of it really matters. The only thing that matters to me is that each day that I was an example of Jesus, and what I did helped someone else come to know Him and get their name written in the Lamb's Book of Life! That is the biggest reason I am writing this book.

My walk has been far from perfect, Christlike, Godly and more. I've made countless mistakes. I've felt like I'm not worthy. The truth is, we are all made in His image. Look:

[27] So God created man in His own image, in the image *and* likeness of God He created him; male and female He created them.

—Genesis 1:27 Amplified Bible (AMP)

I believe that one day we will be in His courtroom. We won't be able to take anything with us, so why do we strive so hard to have the biggest house, the best car, the nicest furniture and so on? All that is material stuff that our flesh requires. Stuff is not of God, it's just stuff. He wants us to trust and be reliant on him. Of course God wants us to have nice things, but also to use those nice things to be an example of Him by giving Him the glory for what we do and what we have. Look:

[9] And I tell you [learn from this], make friends for yourselves [for eternity] by means of the [a]wealth of unrighteousness [that is, use material resources as a way to further the work of God], so that when it runs out, they will welcome you into the eternal dwellings.

Luke 16:9 Amplified Bible (AMP)

It says yes…to further the work of God! It also says if you give, it will be given.

This may sound radical, but to me, it's the truth. We need to make a choice of what's really important to us. Whether you're an educated Christian or a baby Christian, you need to start somewhere. I continue to learn every day. If you need help, many people, including me, are here to help you take the next step. I'll tell you in advance that I don't have all the answers, but together, we can find a renewed understanding that will help us affect the world in a positive and fulfilling way. I promise you, it's not about me. It's about Him and what you can do to glorify Him.

If you'd told me in the third grade that we were made in His image, I would have been extra happy to wear a suit for pictures! Read the Bible to your children. One day, they'll thank you for it.

thirteen

My Child, Drugs And Alcohol

I'm not interested in making friends and building a fan base. I'm interested in telling the truth, seeking the truth and building solution-based programs to help all parents and children who need it.

-Christopher Milo

Between beer commercials, family parties and peer pressure, many of today's children are constantly barraged with images of drugs and alcohol. I grew up with a mom and dad who didn't drink at home or even at family gatherings and parties. I did learn later in my adult life that my father had a serious alcohol problem when he was a young man. Does this have something to do with the generational curses or epigenetic markers?

ep·i·ge·net·ic

͵epijəˈnetik/

adjective

1. Biology

relating to or arising from nongenetic influences on gene expression.

"epigenetic markers"

An easy way to understand, as I continue to learn more about epigenetics every day, is this. Going hand in hand with generational curses, things from our past family members, even from decades ago, are passed down through the gene pool. These bad things leave markers. We have to curse the marker at the root and command them to leave in Jesus' name.

Growing up, I could never understand the craving for alcohol. I remember smelling beer when I was about 8 years old, and it smelled like urine to me. Yuck! My parents always told me it was no good for you. They told me the same thing about drugs. Who was wrong, my parents or all of my musician friends? Most of my family was very musical, so why were they so against alcohol and drugs? You will soon see where I am going with all this.

My father sang opera professionally for thirty-five years. My sister was an accomplished woodwind player. My brother was proficient in the sousaphone, and my mom…she played the radio. Okay, Mom was taking piano lessons while she was pregnant with me. She takes full credit for my musical talents. My father believes I am as talented as I am because he paid for the piano lessons for nine years. That's a family joke; we all know my gifts are from God.

After eleven piano teachers and nine years of piano lessons, I was completely exposed to the world of rock-and-roll. Like most decades, the '80s and '90s were a huge transition period in the music industry, and I was caught deep in the middle of it. It also helped shape how often alcohol and drugs were being used and abused. I've seen it all. Performing with bands all over the USA, I spent more than two decades of my life dealing with peer pressure. "Christopher, drink this, smoke this, sniff this, try this in your arm... you'll feel a little pressure but the rush is great."

I said, "No way! Not a chance! I am out of here!"

As I look back, I'm pleased I had my faith to lean on to keep me straight during the life of sex, drugs and rock-and-roll. I have enough stories to write a book on this topic alone. However, there are some key points I want parents and children to take away from my past and all that I have experienced:

- Be the leader your children need and discuss what is going on currently regarding sex, drugs and alcohol. Don't give them the short version because your kids are getting the tiniest details from among their peer groups at school. Parents, you must define the narrative so your children get the "right" information. Never assume anything, have "the talk," and keep the communication lines wide open!

- Don't ever think your little bundle of joy is innocent. Having trust in your children is awesome, but as a realist, Reagan said it best: "Trust but verify."

- Be careful how lenient you are with your children's electronic devices. I understand that parents can get more things done while your children are occupied, but do not allow your presence to be replaced with electronics. The Internet can be an awesome and powerful tool but it can also be a terrible curse.

- Encourage your children to write, play an instrument, take vocal lessons or read a book.

- Know who your children are talking to over the phone or on FaceTime or Snapchat, especially when they disappear to a different room seeking privacy. Know who they're chatting with on the Internet. Know who they are texting and conversing with through instant messages. Parents say to me all the time, "I don't want my child to not trust me, should they find out I'm invading their privacy." You can't take any chances here. I could write another complete book about all the emails I get from parents whose daughters were abused, whose sons were beaten up and more, all because the parents failed to pay attention to what the kids were doing and didn't create an opportunity to intervene. You are not your child's friend; you are their parent. Your kids will get over it, and if they don't, continue keeping those devices in your possession. Your kids may hate you today, but tomorrow, they will thank you. Stay engaged! I just did an exercise and asked my son Nicholas, who is thirteen, if I could have his phone and look at it. He never answered me; he just handed it to me. I asked him, "Why did you just hand me your phone?" He replied, "I have nothing to hide from you, dad." I asked our ten-year-old, Juliana, the same question and she said, "I have to charge it because it's dead, but you can have it." Ask your kids. If they say no, find out why and what they are hiding. There should be no reason for them not to give it to you upon request. Having a phone or tablet should be viewed as a privilege.

- Limit your kids' access to all social media. You can tell them, "Christopher Milo said so," if you need to relieve yourself from being disliked. Turn the phones off at 7 p.m., so the kids can finish their homework and get ready for bed. If they're being responsible, you as the parent can make a new time.

- Know what programs and websites your children are on. In 2013 alone, I was made aware of 5 suicides in 3 surrounding school districts, all of which traced back to one website where people could impersonate someone else anonymously. This is serious stuff.

- Eat dinner together. If you can't, make a fun face on a paper plate with your kid's name on it. Set it out at the table and leave a loving note for them. Even though you can't be there for whatever reason, they'll still know that you care and wish you could be there.

- Play High/Low with your kids and your spouse. Ask each other what your highs were each day. The high is the best part or the most memorable part of the day. Do the same for the low or the lowest part of the day. This encourages dialogue in the family. All of a sudden, you'll uncover issues that may be bothering your kids.

- When you talk to your kids, close your mouth long enough for your kids to explain what is on their minds. Don't freak out if the information is horrible enough to give you a stroke! If you are the freaking-out kind of parent, I wouldn't want to discuss anything with you either. If what they say warrants disciplinary action, by all means correct them, and then follow it up with love. Be attentive.

- Don't ever hit your child for no reason, even if you think you are being playful. If your dad ripped his belt off his pants and whacked you on the bottom with it, I suggest another alternative. It doesn't matter what we went through as children. Your hands are for picking them up when they fail and fall. Your arms are for holding them when they are crying or feel bummed out for whatever reason.

- Don't allow your children a sense of entitlement. I go to some school districts where ninety percent of the students are on assisted lunches. In another school district twenty miles down the road, ninety percent of the kids could afford to buy the school. I'm not the least bit concerned with your financial situation. Your children need to respect direction and the people giving it. They need to value others' opinions and not think that they are the only blessing God put on this earth.

I take this very seriously. After attending thirty-nine funerals of children under the age of nineteen, I'm not at all interested in making friends or building a fan base. I am interested in telling the truth, seeking the truth and building solution-based programs to assist all parents and children who need help.

The "13 Messages from Milo" is not a cure, it is a solution. If implemented on a daily basis, your entire family will benefit from the results in some way. The only way it can fail is if you fail to follow up and apply the "13 Messages from Milo." Get rid of the markers that were passed down from your parents. Get rid of the markers you passed on to your children. I did.

fourteen

<u>Can This Happen To Me?</u>

I hope you feel my passion to create a solution to the concern.
Not one of us can do it alone.

-Christopher Milo

In 2014 and 2015, I saw an average of 862 students each week. During those two school years, I shared my life's stories during every assembly. No matter how financially stable each community is, the same top questions are discussed. These questions and statements are from students between fourth grade and college.

- "I don't see much opportunity outside the four walls of my school."
- "I'm not very good at anything and my mom was sleeping with every man she met. Where is there room in this life for me?"
- "It's not my fault that I suck, my dad is a loser."

- "My parents don't care."
- "My parents are never around."
- "My parents make good money and give us everything we could ask, but I can't remember the last time my dad threw a ball with me."

These heartfelt comments come from kids just like yours and mine. I don't have all the answers, but in my experience I've discovered a lot of them. My wife, Mary Beth, and I have five children. The kids' ages are ten, thirteen, sixteen, twenty-three and twenty-five. I've spoken to over 100,000 students. Imagine if I could claim them all on my taxes! But all kidding aside, if parents in general were doing their jobs, I'd be in another line of work, rather than sharing these kind of stories with you.

Statistically speaking, eighty-seven of every hundred students I speak with, from fifth grade to high school juniors, tell me there is some type of issue with their parents. I'm not a mathematician, but that's eighty-seven percent of students all saying the same kinds of things. This is the very reason I added a fourth day to my professional mentoring program, dedicating it directly to the parents. As I researched while creating my program, I found not one organization in the states of Ohio, Kentucky, Michigan or Pennsylvania that takes into account direct communication with parents. Amazing! During my program, all parents are invited for an evening meeting so they can better understand what I have been working on with their children during the last 3 visits to the school. Parents have no idea of the things kids are telling me. If they knew what their kids were really saying, they too would be beside themselves.

I had a tenth-grade girl come up to me at the end of an assembly, fighting to get to me on stage. With tears pouring down her face, she knelt down in front of me at my feet screaming, "I'm so sorry, Christopher Milo, I'm so sorry. My parents hate me, that's why I started cutting myself." She lifts up her sleeves and showed the cuts and scars to me and the hundreds of kids around her. "But you've shown me that I can believe in myself! I'm going home today and throwing away all my blades! Thank you, Christopher Milo, thank you." All I did was look up to Heaven, and say "Thank you, God, for blessing me with your words to reach this child."

What really fuels me is that in far too many cases, very few parents show up for my meetings. These meetings are well advertised with fliers and emails that go home to everyone with an email address. I get it; we're all busy. We all have responsibilities. We also cannot afford to miss these engaging, informative meetings at this stage of the game. I make time every week to visit with your children through the day to be a positive influence in their life. I cancel evenings with my family to be with you. When nobody shows up...it is so obvious to me why I am at that school in the first place. It all trickles downhill. If you have a rotten egg in the refrigerator, what happens when you open the fridge? It stinks. When you release that rotten egg out into society, it still stinks. If we don't get rid of the rotten eggs, by nurturing, loving, coaching and counseling our children, nothing is going to change.

This is bigger than the "13 Messages from Milo." This is a movement. This is a community-wide event. This is a statewide endeavor. This is something the entire western hemisphere needs to address. I want everyone to practice the "13 Messages from Milo" every day and teach them to others. Use them in the workplace and in the community you live in. I'm taking them in the schools, but I can only do so much and I could use your help.

It's time we take responsibility for ourselves and our children. We are living in some very broken times. We can't just throw our hands up in the air and give up. Our leadership is broken throughout the country; however, I am still hopeful. There is broken leadership in the school systems of our great country. There is broken leadership in the workplace. What I am asking you to do is this:

Do not allow the leadership in your home to be broken! Together we can break that curse!

Yes, it can happen to you, if you allow it. If every family took responsibility for its own actions, behavior and thoughts, our educational system could worry about educating instead of doing the parents' jobs. Around the country, new testing is being implemented in schools and I promise you the teachers and leadership of the school can't stand it. Add our drug-infested, alcohol-ingested, potty-mouthed, misbehaving, disrespectful children to that mix and what do you get? Exactly. I think you get my point.

I hope you can feel my passion. Please do not take anything I am presenting here personally. If you feel personally offended, you must have an issue that needs fixed. What do you need? How can I be of help to you? I will do my very best to help you or at least connect you with resources in your area. I will look for your email. Please visit www.christophermilo.com and reach out to me.

Every day, I'm in schools that are crying and don't even know what they're crying about. Parents, teachers and administrators ask me the same question over and over again, "Christopher Milo, we tell our students the same types of things that you do; why do they listen to you?"

That one is simple and I have the same reply every time. I am not the parent. I am not the teacher. I'm just a guy who genuinely cares about our youth and uses my own relatable stories to connect with the students. Some educators maintain the same confused look on their face when I say that. I'm only telling you things you most likely already know. Don't you see? It's God's glory light shining through me. It isn't any one thing. The students are making the choice to receive a little blessing that is being given to each of them through me. I am just a vehicle. I am just a man with a huge heart and a love for my Lord and Savior Jesus Christ.

I can't exactly say that in a public school, and I don't because I'm certain it would end my visit. I don't have to say anything. It is in my actions. It is in my presentation and how I carry myself and my humble example that produces the positive fruit. That is exactly what I am asking you to do for your children. Come to one of my school assemblies. Show up at my parent meeting. Be involved. Change your schedule and help me cultivate an environment where the students crave to be and the teachers and administration look forward to going to every day. It affects everyone.

When you receive a blessing like I have, with a second chance with my legs, you want to shout it from the highest mountain. We are all created in His perfect form. If it can happen to me, it can and will happen to you.

Let's pray: *God, I pray for wisdom and clarity. Help me to be outside the norm and help me not to conform to the ways of public school. I pray for each parent and child reading this book that they can learn more about you and the blessings you have for each and every one of us. In Jesus' name I pray; Amen.*

Next Step:
Share this information with all of your closest friends and family members.

fifteen

Trust In Him

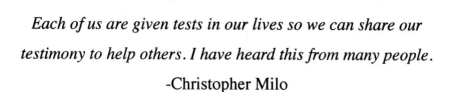

Each of us are given tests in our lives so we can share our testimony to help others. I have heard this from many people.
-Christopher Milo

He has made everything beautiful in its time. He has also set eternity in the human heart; yet no one can fathom what God has done from beginning to end.
Ecclesiastes 3:11

When I was a boy in elementary school, not being chosen to play on a kickball team, I felt like nobody wanted me. I felt as though I would be better off alone. I felt like I didn't matter. I thank my parents for always telling me it was okay and that they loved me. If it weren't for them, I'm not sure how things would have turned out.

I didn't have a walk with God. I was just a kid. We had religion classes, but in my young mind, I was just going through the motions and doing what everyone else did. I had some crazy experiences in first through eighth grade that really made me question my Catholic upbringing. I'd hear one thing from one priest and something different from another. Perhaps it was my own ignorance. Either way, it wasn't until much later that I learned how to trust in Him. I tried. If God was with me in grade school, why did I always get picked last? Why did so many kids pick on me and treat me like I didn't exist and not support the things I was into, like my music? How can I trust in Him?

In high school I was class president and people started to accept me. Was that God or was that my courage growing? I had seen people hurting for one reason or another all throughout my school years. I have always been told, "If it's not good, it's not God." Okay, I can buy that, I guess. But then it got even more confusing. I'd been hurt through relationships. Lied to. Cheated on and betrayed. How was I supposed to trust anyone including Him?

Remember what the verse above says: *He has made everything beautiful in its time*. That says nothing about our time. What we expect is not always what His plan is. God didn't do anything wrong or allow any of those things to happen to me. What God did do was this:

For we are his workmanship, created in Christ Jesus for good works, which God prepared beforehand, that we should walk in them.

Ephesians 2:10

Notice it says **His** workmanship, not Christopher or anyone reading this book, created in Christ Jesus for **good works.**

In simple terms, I went through all the adversity and trials while God watched over me to see what I was going to choose. God prepared beforehand. He knew all along that I would endure the trials that I did and learn how to walk in them, to prepare me for this moment right now. Do you see? If I hadn't gone through everything I went through, what would I write this book about? What would I have to write that could inspire someone else?

Each one of us has a story. Each of us are given tests in our lives so we can share our testimony to help others. We were all blessed with certain gifts. I can tell you this, if everyone on the planet only played the piano, it would drive me nuts! That's why some of us play piano, some of us are in the medical field, some of us work on cars, some of us work in construction and so on.

It's our responsibility to be obedient to Him. Get in his Word (the Bible) and put what we learn into action. We have to budget our time so we can allow time with Him. Nothing else really matters. When I leave this earth, I don't believe I'm going to stop at a toll booth on my way to heaven so I can grab a ticket and check off a list of everything I have accumulated over the years. I don't believe that God's angels will be hanging out saying to each other, "That Milo dude forgot his car payment back in 2010; what a jerk." The way I see it is that we will all be judged by our relationship and walk with Jesus Christ.

When I was little, my father (one of the wisest men I know) used to tell me, "Christopher, don't worry about anything, just be like Jesus and love everybody." I thought, "Are you nuts, dude? People hate me and can't stand that I'm breathing the same air as they are, and you suggest that I should love them?"

That's exactly what to do! My father was correct. All we can do is pray for those who are struggling and lead them to Jesus. Remember Mrs. Meanie Pants in Chapter 10? My flesh wanted to give her a piece of my mind. I immediately asked God for his guidance because I knew I couldn't handle that on my own. Again, He took care of everything.

Don't forget, I was told there was a very good possibility that I would never walk again. Now, more than two decades later, I still have not had a surgery and I still go to the gym. I still build things and do heavy lifting with no pain. Who was right or wrong, the doctors or God?

All through my life people have tried to tell me the truth. I wish I had read this book a long time ago so I could have paid more attention to the signs. For example, once I was performing for an elegant upscale event. The venue was stunning.

I was playing a nine-foot Yamaha concert grand piano. I just started playing my next song, an original. It started out very passionate and emotional. All of a sudden, this guy comes out of nowhere, holding a Bible and screaming in my face like a Baptist preacher. He said, "Young maaaaaan, do ya knooooow what this iiiiiiiis? This is the word of Gaaaaaawd. It is called the BIBLE and it stands for, Basic Instructions Before Leaving Earth. My first thought was "Dude, if you interrupt another one of my songs, I'm calling security." But in the next measure of music, the man was gone.

I am convinced that man was an angel trying to get through my thick head. The signs are all around us. There are so many religions we hear about in our society today. The truth is, what is your relationship with Jesus Christ? That, my friends, is what we will be judged on in His courtroom.

Who do you know that needs help and direction getting to know Jesus Christ? It would take a lot of paper to write over seven billion names so please use this space wisely and write small!

_____

_____

_____

_____

_____

_____

_____

_____

_____

_____

_____

_____

_____

_____

_____

_____

_____

_____

_____

_____

_____

_____

Other than beginning a Bible study at home in your area or finding a Bible-based church, what are some other things you can do to save souls and lead people to Jesus Christ?

_____

_____

_____

_____

_____

_____

_____

_____

_____

_____

_____

_____

_____

What do you need to work on for yourself, before you can help others?

_____

_____

_____

_____

_____

_____

_____

_____

_____

_____

_____

_____

_____

_____

_____

_____

_____

_____

Write down all the things you have to be thankful for.

_____

_____

_____

_____

_____

_____

_____

_____

_____

_____

_____

_____

_____

Write down your personal prayers.

_____

_____

_____

_____

_____

_____

_____

_____

_____

_____

_____

_____

_____

Write a vision statement for yourself.

_____

_____

_____

_____

_____

_____

_____

_____

_____

_____

_____

_____

_____

_____

_____

_____

_____

_____

_____

_____

_____

_____

Write a vision statement for your family.

_____

_____

_____

_____

_____

_____

_____

_____

_____

_____

_____

_____

_____

_____

_____

_____

_____

_____

_____

How do you plan to hold yourself accountable?

_____

_____

_____

_____

_____

_____

_____

_____

_____

_____

_____

_____

_____

_____

_____

_____

Please take the time and the needed self-inventory to answer these questions thoroughly. The first step to success is to create a plan. Once your plan is created, it's time to set realistic goals and then implement your plan. I'm confident you will do well.

sixteen

Preface Questions

"If you want things to change for you, you must change yourself because for every level, there is another devil." I forget who told me this, but it's so true!

-Christopher Milo

If you feel the questions I presented in the Preface were not discussed in enough detail, I am going to detail them now. I first asked the question, "How did each of these scenarios happen?" Let's discuss this from a bird's eye point of view; the big picture.

There is always a cause and effect. There is someone who starts something and someone who finishes it. Here are a few examples for you to noodle on:

1. "He punched me in the face, then received a detention."
2. "She broke up with me and then left town."
3. "I didn't study for my test and received an F."

4. "I failed to call my wife when I left work, and now she's mad."

5. "I've been cutting myself for two years, and my life is falling apart."

I'm going to take notes to show you in other words what else the bullets are saying. Take time to think about whether these apply to you.

1. Aggressive physical behavior. Where did the feeling come from? Do you just show up to work or school and feel angry? Refer to generational curses in chapter 10.

2. Hurtful and broken hearts. What was the cause of the hurt or where did the pain come from?

3. Failing to manage your time and do the things you needed to do. Your job in school is to study and get good grades. Let me tell you a little something. For years, my parents thought I had a learning disability. I didn't have a learning disability; I just didn't care about school. I made a huge mistake. Take your job, which is school, seriously. If you don't, you'll struggle later in life.

4. Expectation. When you tell a friend or your spouse you are going to do something, do it. If you don't, you lose **trust** quickly.

5. Seeking the wrong type of attention. I have met hundreds of students who cut. When we discuss their concerns and

do exercises just like this, every one of them tells me to my face that they are seeking some type of attention from someone.

Is any of this good? Remember: If it's not good, it's not God. There is a pride issue in everything from 1 to 5. Pride is not a good thing. It is okay to be proud of yourself and your accomplishments, or your friends, or your children, but if the only thing you choose to talk about in any setting is yourself, you may want to take your pride to God and discuss it with Him.

In my younger days in high school, I used to walk around fist bumping myself if someone else wasn't around to do it with me. Let's get real for minute. I wrote my first 13-part symphony at the age of 14. Who does that? I could go on and on about my accomplishments but the truth is, who really cares? Do my accomplishments benefit you in any way? Maybe. You may listen to my music and find comfort or a place of peace. Now can I fist bump myself? No! The glory goes to God! Who put me here? My mother? That's a given. Who gave my mother the ability to have me? Her mother? We can go as far back as you want but neither one of us have enough time for that. You will find the One who gets the credit, the One who you should thank, the One who gets the glory, is the One who gave His only son, who died on the cross for our sins and our pride. That sure puts things into perspective, doesn't it? It's not about me! Do you see it now?

In the first example, I present someone getting punched in the face and that someone received a detention for it. I want to break this down to the bare bones for a minute. First, what would cause someone to punch another person in the face? Common sense tells me that that is not the best choice, regardless of whatever caused you to feel the need to do that. For those people who were not blessed with common sense, I'm certain you've heard that punching anyone, for no reason, is not good. That's where you need to start. You need to figure out what's getting you excited or angry enough to want to be aggressive in some way. There is nothing good that comes out of physical violence. Our flesh and our own reasoning made a choice to do something we will most likely regret for one reason or another. After you have a better understanding of your feelings, you will be able to more clearly address the "why" of your actions, and hopefully come up with an alternate solution.

For me, the best resource is the Bible. It has proven to be the best alternate solution in my past and now, the only solution. I prefer the New Living Translation; however, if I feel stumped, I like to read the Amplified version. This scripture, in the book of Numbers, is a great example of cause and effect.

²³ But if you fail to keep your word, then you will have sinned against the LORD, and you may be sure that your sin will find you out.

Numbers 32:23-24 New Living Translation (NLT)

Let's break this down. It says "But if you fail to keep your word;" this is the cause. "Then you have sinned against the Lord;" this is the effect. I want to take this one step deeper for a minute. Parents, how many times have you said to your children, "Don't ever lie to Mommy," or "Truth is better than creativity," or "Lying will make your nose grow." Kids, how many times have you heard something like this? I always wondered where my parents came up with the things they came up with.

For the record the book of Numbers was written by Moses in the plains of Moab, by Jordan, near Jericho sometime between 1405-1444 B.C. People have been using these scriptures for a long time. I am by no means trying to tell you that my parents or your parents are not smart people. I am trying to show you that cause and effect has been around for a very long time. We continue hundreds of years later to deal with this. It also says, "You may be sure that your sin will find you out." That is profound! It says right there that when we sin, He always knows. You may get away with it today or even tomorrow, but God knows exactly what we are doing, every second of every day. The book of Numbers continues in verse 24.

²⁴ Go ahead and build towns for your families and pens for your flocks, but do everything you have promised.

"Do everything you have promised" reminds me of something called the Golden Rule. When I Google this, it says:

gold·en rule

noun

a basic principle that should be followed to ensure success in general or in a particular activity.

"one of the golden rules in this class is punctuality"

the biblical rule of "do unto others as you would have them do unto you" (Matthew 7:12).

noun: **Golden Rule**; plural noun: **Golden Rules**

That Matt fella must have been a swell dude to write something like that! For those that don't understand, I am referring to the book of Matthew in the Bible. He said, "Treat others like you want to be treated."

The morals and principles we try to instill in our children, practice in schools and even the "13 Messages from Milo" are all basics! When I Googled the word "basic," this is what I learned:

ba·sic 'bāsik/

adjective

forming an essential foundation or starting point; fundamental.

"certain basic rules must be obeyed"

noun

the essential facts or principles of a subject or skill.

"learning the basics of the business"

It's critical that we all get back to the basics!

seventeen

Who Do You Reach Out To?

The only reason you will continue to feel alone, is that you
allow yourself to feel that way.
-Christopher Milo

*E*very community has different needs. Every school has different types of concerns, and every home has its own unique function and dysfunction. The good news is that most of you either have direct access to the Internet or know somewhere you can get it, such as your local library. Almost every county has a Chamber of Commerce, which is a form of business network.

There are also hotlines for just about everything. When I meet a student in Nevada with an eating disorder, I Google "help with eating disorder in Nevada." If I am working in the state of Pennsylvania and I meet a student who has a drug addiction, I google "drug help" in the county that I am in. If I'm not successful, I contact the local Chamber of Commerce and ask who they know in the area for this kind of help. The Internet is a powerful tool that can find help quickly when you need it.

When I was younger, we had phone books. These things were larger than *War and Peace*. It took forever to find something you needed. If you have a smartphone or other smart device, you can find anything you need in a matter of seconds if you know what keywords you're looking for.

Friends and family are also a good resource. If you call Aunt Suzy and share with her what is going on, you may quickly learn that you have more resources than you realized. Your local church may be another great resource. I believe in the power of prayer. Maybe Aunt Suzy doesn't, but the stranger you just met at your local church will be sure to offer up prayers and you can count on them contacting other church members to help pray. You haven't seen anything until you watch a prayer chain in action. These people will not judge you, but will genuinely bring your concerns up to the Almighty.

Know this. You are never alone. More often than not, I meet parents, students or teachers who will say, "Nobody understands what I am going through; I feel so alone." If you want to keep your concerns to yourself, then you will remain alone.

I have never met anyone that can do anything great all by themselves. For example, *"Born on July 30, 1863, near Dearborn, Michigan, Henry Ford created the Ford Model T car in 1908 and went on to develop the assembly line mode of production, which revolutionized the industry. As a result, Ford sold millions of cars and became a world-famous company head."* Do you think he did this by himself? No way! He had a team of people helping him try new things. Do you think he failed? Of course he did and so did his team.

Have you ever heard of a guy by the name of Martin Luther King, jr.? *"(January 15, 1929 – April 4, 1968) was an American Baptist minister and activist who was a leader in the African-American civil rights movement. He is best known for his role in the advancement of civil rights using nonviolent civil disobedience based on his Christian beliefs."* He had many people working with him. There is no way someone can move a community and affect the world by him- or herself.

Here is one more. *LeBron Raymone James (/lə'brɒn/; born December 30, 1984) is an American professional basketball player for the Cleveland Cavaliers of the National Basketball Association (NBA). James played high school basketball at St. Vincent–St. Mary High School in his hometown of Akron, Ohio, where he was highly promoted in the national media as a future NBA superstar. In 2016, The Cleveland Cavaliers won the NBA Championship breaking the 52-year drought.* Do you think LeBron won that by himself? Of course not. There are many players on the team that contribute to the success of LeBron. The team is called the Cleveland Cavaliers, not the Cleveland

LeBron. Nothing great happens alone. However, every great thing begins with an idea!

If you have a concern, take charge and fix it. The only reason you will continue to feel alone is that you allow yourself to feel that way.

Write down your next great idea, and an action plan that includes the next steps to bring it to life!

_____

_____

_____

_____

_____

_____

_____

_____

_____

_____

_____ .

eighteen

How do kids and parents deal with life's circumstances?

Life is like a new composition, you take it one musical note at a time, see what you can do in harmony with other notes, then share it with the world.

-Christopher Milo

Throughout my life, I have tried to handle life's circumstances on my own. I am sad to report that every time I did this, I failed completely. My flesh has gotten in the way throughout my life. The Devil has taken over at times and nothing good has ever come out of anything when my flesh, my ideas, my desires and actions are done without seeking Him first.

During my younger years, I did what many other kids did. I attempted to follow the trends, tried to figure out where I fit in and at whatever level I did things, I just accepted where I was at the time. Both children and adults have asked me, "How did you become so talented on the piano and how do you play so fast?" I used to say that I practice a lot, and when you're good, you're good. The truth is, I have played an estimated fifty billion notes in my career so far and I have messed up half of them. With God protecting my hands and my emotions, I get better and better every day. That's how I now reply.

Life is like a new composition, you take it one musical note at a time, see what you can do in harmony with other notes, then share it with the world. There are some people in the world who create things. There are some people in the world who pay for things. There are some people in the world who cheer for things.

For example, take Game 7 of the 2016 NBA finals. In this example, the hard work, dedication and competitiveness of the Cleveland Cavaliers and the Golden State Warriors created Game 7. There are wealthy people who paid for the Oracle Arena so there was a venue available to play basketball. Thousands of fans showed up to that history-making game and cheered for their favorite team. What if they had had to play outside somewhere and had no arena? What if nobody showed up for the game? Do you think the energy would have been the same?

I will always remember that game. I was at home with my wife and kids, screaming at the top of my lungs during the last two minutes. After Kyrie Irving swished a three-point shot and LeBron James made one of two foul shots, it put the Cavs up by four points with only seconds left on the clock. The tears poured out of every eye in my house. I promise you this, even if you don't like basketball or didn't see the game, you at least heard about it for the next few days. That game will go down in history, and people will talk about it for however long forever lasts.

It doesn't matter if you are an NBA professional or a kid like me with no one to listen to my music; we all need support. We all need the tools to be successful. We all need help at some point, in some way. Many of the students I coach have issues with drugs, alcohol, self-harm, being picked on or abused, sports issues, academic issues and more. I have learned something very powerful. If your support system is able to display the traits of the "13 Messages from Milo," your solution is well on its way. If you choose to seek God before you do anything, I am confident your solution will be given. He gave me mine.

So how do kids and parents deal with life's circumstances? The answer to that will come when you create a relationship with God's son, Jesus Christ. Read the Bible. You may not understand immediately but supernaturally, things will be revealed to each and every one of His children. There is nothing to lose. His love never fails.

I asked one more question. Why does this happen to my family? I encourage you to join a good Bible-based church. I also encourage you to look deeper into epigenetics and generational curses. Please know this: I have never met a perfect family or individual that has never experienced some type of failure. If you're out there, please send me an email; I'd love to meet you. You can continue to ask the question why or you can invest your energy on how to fix it. It all goes back to choices. There is only one perfect choice. I pray you make it.

What are some choices you want to make that will improve your life?

_____

_____

_____

_____

_____

_____

_____

_____

_____

_____

_____ .

nineteen

Thoughts And Ideas

Sweetheart?

-Christopher Milo

I've enjoyed sharing my thoughts and experiences with you. I hope and pray that you'll use this book as a tool for your own personal growth and development. I want you to revisit the chapters and the notes you wrote down as you see yourself grow personally and spiritually. I hope you find the information relatable and use this book as well as your own stories to impact someone else. Revisit the questions in this book when you start your own small groups. All you need is the desire, some paper, pencils and the "13 Messages from Milo" written down so others can see them. Schools have them hanging up all over their hallways. Businesses have them individually hanging around offices. Bullying needs to be eliminated from the English language and will not be tolerated. Dislike is replaced with like.

Abuse become useable. Respect becomes a priority and a love and passion for Jesus is really all that matters. Thank you God for giving me the experiences you have given me so we could write this book together. I thank you for giving me my legs back so I could sit up and write this book.

I want to touch on the words judging and drama. I am a perfect target for someone to judge. I have learned to enjoy it actually. People from every community look at me like I have lost my mind when they see my Mohawk hair style. Some people have asked me if I like the attention. The attention I enjoy is when someone stops me and asks what type of product I use in my hair. I kindly answer their question and always add, "and I shaved my head to honor children battling pediatric cancer." After the uncomfortable pause, they wipe the shame off their faces. In short, I lovingly explain my story.

We have to remember that everyone has a story. The skinny girl may be skinny because she has an eating disorder. The overweight gentleman isn't overweight because he loves it; maybe he has a thyroid issue that he is trying to get under control. The kid that sits next to you in school might have a sad look on their face because they failed a test that they studied very hard for, or maybe because their parent got shipped off to war. They are not mad at you like you think. I'll say this until I can't say it any more: we make judgements about others, based on little to no information. That's wrong on so many levels. We need to pray for the people who are like that! I hope that is clear!

Oh wait. Remember that in the preface of the book, I told you I would explain what bullying meant? In the 1500's the word meant "Sweetheart." At the turn of the 1700's the word dissipated and just went away. Today, we know it as being in some type of imminent danger. Really? Stop using it. We have misconstrued the meaning of the word so much over the last several hundred years that nobody gets it. From school to school, it means something a little different. If we stop using it and replace it with something kind, respectful and loving, maybe it will go away. Let's make up our own word. Do you have any suggestions?

_____

_____

_____

_____

_____

_____

_____

_____

_____

_____

<u>twenty</u>

<u>Messages To Use And Weekly Planner</u>

Please use this in some way!
-Christopher Milo

As my program has become more popular in different communities and school districts, the need for additional follow-up has become much greater. After I've been to a school four, eight, twelve or more times, it's critical to keep my messages in front of the students or employees. Often, I'll follow up with a school and see bulletin boards full of the "13 Messages from Milo" in very creative ways. Huge posters hang from balconies in schools with student art and interpretation of what each message means to them. Businesses take photos of employees showing each one of the messages. It's beautiful to see the creativity in all the places I go.

Follow-up is the key to my program. Businesses use my messages in morning meetings and schools get even more

182

creative. I can Skype into a school, record my messages on CD or even assist teachers in writing morning messages to share each week with students and staff. Although I've received hundreds of written messages from teachers, there's one particular school that stands out. That is St. Francis Xavier in Medina, Ohio. The teachers included Bible verses that are relevant to each one of my messages. These were read over the loudspeaker in school every Monday so the students could get refreshed and be prepared for the week.

I want to share these messages with you in this book. I invite you to use these messages in your business or school. I also invite you to customize each message for your specific needs.

A special thanks to the staff and administration at St. Francis Xavier School in Medina, Ohio!

Weekly Messages with Scripture:
These can be read before the group/lesson starts, as well as being copied and sent home with students to share with their families. This encourages interaction with the family and gives the opportunity for the student to practice reading aloud. I ask you to take notes in the space provided. As a school, business, or family, look for ways to make each topic better. When you have been through all thirteen, start over and review your notes from each week. I trust you'll see improvement, no matter what environment you are in.

WEEK_____ BE POSITIVE

Dear Students,

What a great week this is going to be! I am excited that you'll be using my "13 Messages from Milo" in the weeks to come. This week, we are going to kick this off with **"BE POSITIVE."** In my experience, I have seen wonderful positive examples from students of all ages. I understand that every day may not be a perfect day. However, each day will be as good as you choose to make it. During the weeks to come, I'm going to touch on many different things but most important, I'm going to include Scripture from the Bible to reinforce the points I'm going to make. Pay attention to your actions, to how you choose to react to things and most importantly, to how you act in front of others. Be a good example in the eyes of God and be a wonderful example to others. I look forward to sharing a message with you each week! Be blessed!

Christopher Milo

_____

_____

_____

_____

WEEK _____LOVE ONE ANOTHER

Dear Students,

I want to welcome you to another great week. I understand that this week you will be focusing on my message "**LOVE ONE ANOTHER**". In John 13:34, we hear "I give you a new commandment. As I have loved you, so you also should love one another." We know that Jesus was asking us to love our brothers and sisters across racial and ethnic groups, love the weakest and the strongest, love the old and the young, love the disabled and the troublemakers. In looking at this message, I want you to focus this week on how you can serve others. How can you help out a friend, classmate, your parents, or someone in your community? When you help others and love one another you impact everyone around you. Take action, and you can make a change in your school, class, community, and your world. I challenge you to go do fantastic things this week for those around you. I can't wait to hear from your adult leaders what great things you do this week.

Christopher Milo

WEEK_____TRUST

Dear Students,

Welcome back to another great week at_____. I understand that this week you will be focusing on my message **"Trust."** Trusting one another is a powerful thing, whether it is trusting your family, friends, teachers, etc. Trust involves relying on one another and on our integrity, and also means having confidence in one another. Trust is the foundation of our friendships and our relationships. Without trust, you wouldn't have as strong of community as you do here in Medina. This week, I want you to remind yourselves of who you trust in your own lives and reflect upon the question **"What can I do to become a more trustworthy and trusting person?"** It is also important to always remember to trust in God, as he is the one who continues to guide us through life. One of my favorite scriptures, which I recite before every performance, is Proverbs 3:5-6. It reminds us to "Trust in the Lord with all your heart and lean not on your own understanding; in all your ways, submit to Him, and he will make your paths straight."

I look forward to hearing about all of the amazing ways you are continuing to build and show trust within your community this week and in the weeks to come. I am very pleased to hear the wonderful reports coming in from the adult leaders! Keep up the great work!

Christopher Milo

_____

_____

_____

_____

_____

_____

_____

_____

_____

_____

_____

_____

_____

_____

_____

_____

_____

_____

_____

_____

_____

_____

_____

_____

_____

_____

_____

_____

_____

_____

_____

_____

WEEK_____WORK TOGETHER

Dear Students,

Welcome back to another awesome week! My message that you will be focusing on this week is **"Work together."** There are so many opportunities for us to work together in our lives as Jesus has taught us. In Paul's letter to the Romans, he tells us "May the God of endurance and encouragement grant you to live in such harmony with one another, in accord with Christ Jesus, that together you may with one voice glorify the God and Father of our Lord Jesus Christ." (15:5-6.)

In school you can help classmates with work that they do not understand. At home, work together with your family to help clean up the house or yard…without someone asking. Work with your teachers and do as they ask so that the classroom will run smoothly and everyone can learn new things together. Most important, work together with God by praying and reflecting on your actions and trying to be the best version of yourself that you can be. Matthew 9:26 says "With God all things are possible." So work with those around you and not against them. When we work together, we can all accomplish great things.

Christopher Milo

WEEK____ACCEPT

Dear Students,

Good morning! I want to welcome you back to another wonderful week. I'm told that this week you will be focusing on my message "**Accept.**" Ephesians 4:2 tells us, "with all humility and gentleness, with patience, accepting one another in love." We know that we need to accept all people regardless of any differences we might have with others. It doesn't matter if someone listens to the same music, or plays the same sport as you; everyone deserves to be accepted. To accept someone is to give validation and show respect for who they are and what they do. When you show acceptance toward someone, you're giving them a positive feeling about who they are. I want to encourage each and every one of you to go throughout this week, and make someone feel better about who they are; I want you to be accepting of everyone around you.

Christopher Milo

_____

_____

_____

_____

WEEK____USE YOUR TALENTS

Dear Students,

Good morning and welcome back to another great week. My message that you will be focusing on this week is "Using your talents." In 1 Peter 4:10 we hear that each of us has received a gift to use to serve one another as good stewards of God's varied grace. God gives each of us gifts, not because we have earned it, but because He is so gracious. With the giving of this gift comes responsibility. Don't waste your gift. Use it well. What is your talent? Perhaps you have a musical talent that you could use to bring joy to others. Maybe you are good at math, writing, acting, or playing a sport. Whatever your talent is, find some way to share it for the benefit of others. If we all used our gifts for the sake of others, what a wonderful world this would be. So this week, focus on using your talent to improve the quality of someone else's life.

Christopher Milo

WEEK____BE CREATIVE

Dear Students,

I hope you had a great week. My message for this week is **"Be Creative."** We know from the Book of Genesis that we are made in the image and likeness of God. God, the Creator, has given us the gift of creativity. When we use our creative abilities, we are mirroring God's work of creation.

You may think this just applies to people who can draw, play music, paint or write stories, but it means so much more. One of my favorite quotes, by Albert Einstein, is "Creativity is intelligence having fun." Just as there are all different types of intelligence, there are all different types of creativity. You may not be an artist or musician, but you may be able to come up with a new way to work a math problem or solve a conflict. You might create a new app or computer game, develop a new play on the field, or find a new way to explain something to someone who doesn't understand. Whatever your creative gift may be, have fun with it and remember to use it for the good of others!

Christopher Milo

WEEK_____INSPIRE

Dear Students,

I hope you're looking forward to a great week. Your message for this week is to **Inspire**. The definition of "inspire" is "to influence or impel; or to guide or control, be divine influence." The Greek translation of the word inspiration literally means God-breath. Clearly God is our inspiration in everything we do.

It is now our turn to inspire others by our actions. We need to think about being Christlike in our actions. Are you kind to others? Do you encourage them? Do you help them to look for their best qualities and use them? Inspire others to be positive in all they do. Do you inspire the people in your life who are not religious to seek God and to have a relationship with Him? Young people can be the best inspiration to the older people in their life. It is our responsibility to teach everyone we meet about God. Your awesome example will show Christ in you for others to see. Remember: If it's not good, it's not God! Take a minute to do something to inspire the people you come into contact with this week.

Christopher Milo

WEEK_____COACH

Dear Students,

Welcome back to another fun-filled week! This week you'll focus on my message of **"Coach."** God calls us to coach and lead others along the path of the Lord. We can do this in our everyday lives by coaching classmates on how to do things. Don't just tell them how to do a problem or what to do, but show them. Coaching them on the correct way to do it, just as a coach shows you how to do something in a sport.

Colossians 3:23-24 says, "Whatever you do, work at it with all your heart, as working for the Lord, not for men, since you know that you will receive an inheritance from the Lord as a reward. It is the Lord Christ you are serving." In coaching others to improve, you are serving God. While we can serve God by coaching others, we must also be open to being coached by others. Listen to your coaches in the sports that you play or the activities that you are involved in, just like this one. The leaders in this group are dedicating their time and energy to you and making you better. We can all improve in everything that we do and no one is perfect except for God. Use your coaches to your advantage and work to improve your life and better serve the Lord.

Christopher Milo

WEEK____BE CURIOUS

Dear Students,

Hello! Welcome back to another awesome week! I understand that this week you will be focusing on my message **"Be Curious."** Living with curiosity is very important. Curiosity drives the mind and allows you to become more observant about so many new ideas and things in this world that God has given to us. Curiosity allows us to become active learners in school, opens up a world of creativity and imagination that we may have never experienced, and it brings so much more excitement into our lives. Living with curiosity can be done in so many different ways, whether it may be attempting a new science experiment, trying out for a new sport that you may not be familiar with, or exploring a new way to solve a math problem. Being curious also encourages you to ask those "why" questions, which allows you to think critically about the topics you may be studying in school or about the world around you. Some of our world's greatest scientists, philosophers and mathematicians, became great not because they were so intelligent but because they lived with curiosity. As Albert Einstein once said, "I have no special talents. I am only passionately curious."

I look forward to hearing about all of the amazing ways you continue to embody and live out my messages in your own lives. Keep up the great work!

Christopher Milo

_____

_____

_____

_____

_____

_____

_____

_____

_____

_____

_____

_____

_____

_____

_____

_____

_____

_____

WEEK____LISTEN

Dear Students,

I want to welcome you back to another great week. I understand that this week you will be focusing on my message, **"Listen."** This is one of the most respectful qualities a person can show to others. James 1:19 says, "Understand this, my beloved brothers and sisters. Let everyone be quick to hear [be a careful, thoughtful listener], slow to speak [a speaker of carefully chosen words and], slow to anger [patient, reflective, forgiving]."

God wants us to Listen. When we listen, we pay attention. When we pay attention, we show respect. When we show respect, we show love. It all works together. I trust that everyone who hears this message will work on being the best listener in the group! Have an amazing week!

Christopher Milo

_____
_____
_____
_____
_____

WEEK____COMMUNICATE

Dear Students,

Hello! I want to welcome you back to another great week. I'm told that this week you will be focusing on my message **"Communicate."** Communication is so important among people. Our words are very powerful. They can hurt or they can encourage; they can build, or they can tear down. Whether we're communicating in speech or in writing, we should seek to be blessings to whomever we come in contact with. Many of you are communicating with one another by text messaging. The great aspects of text messaging are that it is quick and easy. The bad aspects are that it can be used to bully and harass others. In Ephesians 4:29 we read, "Let no corrupting talk come out of your mouths, but only such as is good for building up, as fits the occasion, that it may give grace to those who hear." God wants us to build each other up, not tear each other down, and remember...your words will affect someone. Choose your words wisely so they can be used for good instead of being hurtful! This week, be Godly examples by communicating with words that are uplifting.

Christopher Milo

WEEK____BE GENUINE

Good morning! I hope you are enjoying your last weeks of school and are determined to finish strong! The last of my 13 messages is "Be Genuine." This means being sincere, honest and true to yourself. God made each of us a unique, one-of-a-kind individual with our own special talents and abilities. In Psalm 139 we hear, "You formed my innermost being; you knit me in my mother's womb. I praise you, so wonderfully you made me. Your eyes foresaw my actions; in your book all are written down."

God has a plan for us and we need to be true to who we are so we can follow the path He has laid down for us. I know from personal experience how great the pressure can be to fit in and follow the crowd. But I can also tell you that I would not have the happiness, fulfillment and purpose in my life if I had abandoned my music in order to feel accepted. Remember how nobody wanted to listen? My music is now heard in 43 countries around the globe. Thank you, Jesus! So, always strive to be genuine, for as the saying goes, "Be yourself; the original is always worth more than a copy." You guys are awesome! I look forward to seeing you all again!

Christopher Milo

13 Messages from Milo

13 Week Planner

Week of: **Message:**

(Example)

March 14ᵗʰ,   *2010*   *Be Positive*

Week of:	Year	Message:
_____	20____	Be Positive
_____	20____	Love One Another
_____	20____	Trust
_____	20____	Work Together
_____	20____	Accept
_____	20____	Use Your Talents
_____	20____	Be Creative
_____	20____	Inspire
_____	20____	Coach
_____	20____	Be Curious
_____	20____	Listen
_____	20____	Communicate
_____	20____	Be Genuine

Be Positive

Love One Another

Trust

Work Together

Accept

Use Your Talents

Be Creative

Inspire

Coach

Be Curious

Listen

Communicate

Be Genuine

twenty-one

We Are A Spirit First

"I learn every day as my walk with Him continues"
-Christopher Milo

Here are some notes for you to process:

We are a spirit first. We have a soul, will, mind and emotion and live in a body. Our spirit, which is eternal, has an eternal father, God or the Devil. We are a spirit first living in our bodies for a short time. Sin can't live in heaven. Our spirit will never die. Every person lives eternally.

God sent his son to take our sins to the cross, to pay for our sins. The Word says that when we go to heaven, we are going home. Our spirits are eternal. Our soul; what does that do? Does it go to heaven? We live out of our souls. If we feed it spiritual food, we will behave like Christ. If we feed it earthly things, we lust after the worldly things that God hates. We need to speak it, live it and be it. Our spirits are designed to live eternally. If you become born again and live the life of Christ, you will go to heaven.

Questions:

Do you even know what you are choosing?

It's your choice. What will you choose?

Let's try to process this:

We are an eternal spirit and our spirit never dies. It will always live.

We are a spirit, with a soul, that lives in this body.

Our body is not eternal. It typically can't live more than about 90-100 years, but our spirit is eternal and it will live forever. We have a choice here on earth of where we will spend eternity. Our spirits serve either the Devil or our Father God and our spirit will do the will of whoever's will we serve. If you don't serve the Father in heaven, then you automatically serve the Devil and don't even know it.

I didn't know it until I read the Bible.

Once we learn about what Jesus did for us and get reborn again, we can go to heaven. Jesus was without sin and was the perfect sacrifice. He took all our sins to the cross so we can go to heaven. Jesus is fully God and fully man.

You can ask Jesus to forgive your sins and ask Him to please be your Lord and savior. We can confess with our mouths and believe in our hearts that He died and after three days, he was raised from the dead and sits on the right side of the Father. Our spirit will be reborn again and we can live for eternity in heaven. Praise God!

Remember we are a spirit, we have a soul, and we live in a body.

twenty-two

Have You Been In Prison Too?

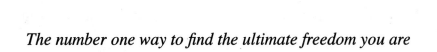

The number one way to find the ultimate freedom you are looking for is to remember this; If it's not good, It's not God.

-Christopher Milo

There were many years of my life that I chose to leave out of this book for various reasons. Maybe one day I will write the rest of my story, but for now I'll leave you with this. For the young people reading this book, I want you to understand that growing up over the years, I did not always make the right choices. I have learned from my mistakes and other people's mistakes. I have experienced a life of success and a life of failure. I have seen a life of misunderstanding and a life of happiness. I have been faced with the choice of doing drugs or not doing drugs. I have been tested with choosing alcohol or no alcohol at all. I have been faced with being the bully or choosing to walk away. I have made the choice to not jump when jumping seemed like the best solution.

If you ask a soldier what freedom means, that person will talk about fighting for the beautiful country they live in. If you ask a Nascar driver to tell you the definition of freedom, they might tell you a story about driving down an open country road and not having any place to be. If you ask a homeless person the same question, they will tell you about having enough meals to last longer than a day. If you ask a person addicted to drugs, opioids or alcohol, they will most likely tell you that freedom means to escape from the life they are currently in and may even describe freedom as death. No matter what situation you are in, the definition of freedom for every scenario I described can be two simple words: Jesus Christ.

I had religion in my life while I was growing up. What I didn't have was a relationship with Jesus. You may or may not have religion or a relationship with Jesus, but I can tell you it is never too late to begin a relationship with Jesus, no matter your current age or offense. I have seen some of the most profound testimonies over the years from people who "lost it all" in their own way and still won the battle they were in. I know people who have had miraculous cures from cancer and other terminal illnesses. I know addicts and alcoholics who have received their complete healing and now help others with the same concerns they once had. I have witnessed with my own eyes instant healings in young people with all types of issues.

How? The answer is Jesus.

I was in my own prison. A prison of loneliness, stuck in my own head with a daily regimen that consisted of "hurry up and wait," then repeat. What kind of life is that, and who wants to live that kind of life? What kind of mind chooses to stay stuck like that? I am here to tell you that when I didn't have Jesus, I was a miserable person, a mean person and more. I was lost and alone. I felt that if I did not exist, life would be better for everyone else.

Your current walk may be better or worse than mine as you read this book. It really doesn't matter. What matters to me is that you find the same thing I did and experience the same love and joy that I walk in every day. You are the reason I wrote this book. Your concerns have inspired me to help others. We both have made mistakes, but it doesn't mean we don't deserve to be happy. You matter to me. You are important. You are worth it. I may not know you personally, but I can promise you that I have met someone like you, or the me that I once was.

I was blessed with a second chance and I am writing this prayer for you now:

I decree and declare that the person reading this book receives their complete healing, Lord. I pray that abundant blessings shower the reader. I pray that your unemployed angels

*work overtime for my new friend reading this, and they are pro-
tected and feel safe and secure, God. I pray that they have open
visions and open their eyes, God, to your marvelous work of
healings and miracles. I pray in Jesus' name, Father God that
the lost will be found, and I command all evil spirits to leave this
reader, in Jesus' name. I love you Lord. Thank you, Jesus, for
shedding your blood on the cross that paid for our sins. Thank
you, Heavenly Father, for teaching us that if it's not good, it's
not God. In Jesus' name I pray. Amen.*

And for the adults who are reading this, I ask each of you
to grant me one wish. If this book has blessed you in any way,
please use it to bless someone else. It could be a friend, a family
member, someone at work or a stranger who you see in passing
when you get your coffee at your local coffee shop tomorrow.
This information is no good if we don't share it. Practice the
"13 Messages from Milo" with your own family. Make up your
own curriculum with this book as the foundation for the home or
your place of business. Be a leader for your children. If you're
the one who's lost, get rid of your pride and find help now. I
know it's hard to do, but if I can do it, so can you. I have worked
with thousands of parents who thought they had all the right
answers, but the reality was that they were the ones who were
most lost. Take the daily self-inventory you deserve to take and
look for areas of opportunities both for yourself and your children. It is a simple choice. I pray you make a good one.

Maybe I will see you on the streets. Maybe I will see you in your child's school or in your parents' nursing home. If I don't, I hope I at least see you in Heaven, and the only way that's going to happen is if you and your family accept Jesus into your life. Hell is for real, my friends. You don't have to believe me if you don't want to, but why risk it! I'll pray I see you soon.

What are some positive changes can you make in your life?

_____

_____

_____

_____

_____

_____

_____

_____

_____

_____

_____

_____

_____

_____

_____

_____

_____

_____

_____

_____

_____

_____

_____

_____

_____

_____

_____

_____

_____

_____

_____

_____

_____

P.S. I dare you to share this book with 50-500 other people. You just might be the blessing they have been searching for.

twenty-three

My New Beginning

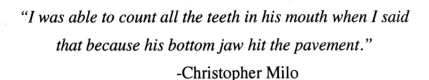

"I was able to count all the teeth in his mouth when I said
that because his bottom jaw hit the pavement."
-Christopher Milo

Now that you have successfully made some awesome changes in your life, it is time to take some new steps. Don't look behind you; look in front of you. There's nothing you can do to change the past, but your choices, moving forward, can brighten your future. Look for the good in others. Give people room to not be perfect. Before I was saved, I would look at things much differently than I do now. If my wife burned the toast when making me breakfast, I would have looked at the burned toast and reminded her that I can't be late for work. In my angry mind, I might have created opportunities to correct her on various things in which I felt differently about. As a saved man, burned toast creates a few more minutes to admire my wife and all of her abundant beauty. I can use that time to be a blessing to her while the fresh bread is in the toaster. I can get back to what I was doing soon enough.

I made a life choice and so should you! My choice is to react differently to things. Focus on the good qualities of someone else and stop trying to change people. We become so involved with our flesh and worldly things that we often fail to see the goodness that is right in front of our faces. Don't invest your time comparing yourself, your spouse or your children to everyone else. I can almost promise you that the person you are comparing yourself to is dealing with their own weaknesses, just like you and I are. Instead of complaining to your children about all the things they don't do, try praising them for the things they do well. Stop telling them the things you don't like and replace your words with loving compliments. Tell another person how much you appreciate them for something instead of pointing out all of the faults. I don't know about you, but I respond to praise much better than I do someone criticizing me for this or that. The same respect and honor you wish you had on a daily basis is the same honor and respect you need to show.

Here is a great example for you. My wife got home the other day from her morning run. I was deep in my work, and any interruption at this point could be devastating, with my current deadlines. However, with all the many things she has to do, her time is not always budgeted very well. She could see I am in the middle of doing something, but asked me if I could make her two poached eggs. This could go down one of two ways. I could tell her I was in the middle of something, and she would be just fine with that and manage her time the best she could. She would rush around and figure it out. However, based on countless breakfasts together, I know in the back of my mind that beginning her day that way would not be the best. Or, I could tell her that I would be happy to make her eggs, set aside what I am doing for a few minutes, even if it is the solution for world peace, and make her eggs. I replied to her with a loving tone that I would be happy to make her eggs. She smiled and went about her morning less rushed, full of joy, feeling loved and like she matters.

How we react to people, how we act towards people and the tone of voice we choose in our reply, will set the mood for the next minute, hour or day. I challenge you to try reacting in a Godly manner every day with your children, your parents, your co-workers or anyone else you come in contact with. What you say or do to someone today could change their life in some way. The key to doing this is to be attentive and patient to what is going on around you. Remove the focus from yourself! Of course whatever it is that you are doing at that moment is most important and I am sure the "not filled with Christ" person makes everyone know that. This is why when you do something like I did when I made the eggs for my wife, she appreciated those eggs more than anything. She said thank you with a smile, was able to slow down for a moment and was very kind and loving. That reminds me of a scripture in the Bible:

[4] Love is patient, love is kind. It does not envy, it does not boast, it is not proud. [5] It does not dishonor others, it is not self-seeking, it is not easily angered, it keeps no record of wrongs. [6] Love does not delight in evil but rejoices with the truth. [7] It always protects, always trusts, always hopes, always perseveres.

[8] Love never fails.

—1 Corinthians 13:4-8New International Version (NIV)

That to me is profound! It sums up everything I "showed" my wife and told you in my story. I can assure you, before I had Jesus in my heart, my egg story would have been told in a very different way. I am learning every day to look ahead and be a blessing to others.

Here is another blessing for you:

My wife and I visit our local grocery store at least two times a week. For months, I would walk in and out of the store and see the same gentleman pushing carts in the parking lot. When I saw him, I observed him moving very slowly. He never smiled at anyone. He looked as though he felt very unappreciated. Weeks went by and I continued to see this gentleman pushing carts with little to no urgency at all. Finally, one day I went to the grocery store to grab something really quick. I saw this man pushing carts right when I pulled in the parking lot. I parked, shut my eyes and said, "God, please give me the words to be a blessing to this man. I pray in Jesus' name. Amen." I got out of my vehicle. He was three parking spots away from me. I was nervous. What was I going to say to him? Oh boy!

As I approached him I said, "Hi, my name is Christopher. What's your name?" In a soft tone he replied, "My name is Duane." I said, "Nice to meet you, sir." while extending my hand towards his. When we shook hands, I said, "I've seen you here for weeks. I see how hard you work, and every time you're here, I never have to worry if there is a cart for me inside. I really appreciate you! I just wanted to say thank you for what you do here."

I was able to count all the teeth in his mouth when I said that because his bottom jaw hit the pavement. You could see his facial expression change from death to life. It was like he stood up from a lifetime of sitting down. Every time I went to the store after that and still to this day, Duane and I greet each other with a smile.

What Duane doesn't know is that it was uncomfortable for me to greet him. If I didn't pray and put God first before I said what I said, I probably would have walked by him, just like everyone else. He is a blessing to me. He provides a cart for me in the hot summer, the rainy spring and snowy winter, every time I shop. I am very grateful for him.

Who can you encourage today? Who can you bless today in some way? One random act of kindness or simple smile could change someone's life forever, just like Duane did for me.

Something else I want you to focus on during this new beginning is to accept others and their differences. I encourage you to meet people where they are at. Don't try to change people. If you invest your time trying to change people and you are not successful, you will feel defeated and possibly even grow to resent that person.

My wife, Mary Beth, likes to sit on the right side of the couch when we do a Bible study or watch one of our favorite Christian shows. I love to sit on the right side of the couch because I'm right-handed and the end table is next to the couch where I can place my drink. Much of my happiness comes from watching her be content. Seeing that she is comfortable and feeling relaxed is far more important to me than selecting the perfect place in the living room to sit down.

The result, is I say nothing at all and accept the fact that the right side of the couch is hers. Instead of resenting her or saying anything, I am just grateful we have a couch to sit on. I could fight, scream, punch, bark and bite, but that will get us nowhere! Pretty simple, isn't it? If it isn't simple to you, I recommend you invest more time in prayer and reading the Bible!

Something else that it is important to me is that you experience "loving yourself" and "loving others." Have you ever heard the saying "actions speak louder than words?" I can look at one of my children a certain way and they will know if they forgot to turn the light off in the other room. They will also know if I am pleased with them by the look on my face. The real question is this. Are you looking attentively enough at your children to recognize that there may be a concern that needs to be addressed? I know it isn't always easy to show love. Some of the choices our children make are not always easy to accept; however, accepting is exactly what we need to do. Your goals may be different from your child's goal. This is where "loving" comes into play.

My son Nicholas is a perfect candidate for playing football. He is thirteen years old, the right height, and fast. His leg press is greater than many adults'. He loves all sports but playing football is not on the top of his priority list. My goal for him would be to play football but his goal is to play basketball. As his father, I need to encourage him, share my opinions as to why I think he should play football and then let him and God decide what to do. I have to remember that Nicholas is the one that would be getting pounded on the football field, not me. I also need to remember that with God in control, Nicholas will make the best choice for Nicholas. I will love him no matter what he chooses to do. As parents, we can't love our children or our spouses without accepting them where they are. We need to love them for who they are. Love is not dictated by what will happen in your time, or your standards. I need to love Nicholas for who God created him to be, not what I think he should be. It's about God's plan, not mine. My job as his father is to keep encouraging him to do great things and let God do the rest.

Communication is a key component in all of this. We need to be satisfied with what we have and not be frustrated with what we don't have. I have never met anyone who has one hundred percent perfect qualities. We need to accept our children, our spouses and extended family and friends for who they are and the people they are striving to become, just like I am trying to do with Nicholas.

These are some basic suggestions that I hope you take to heart. I remember when I was reborn again in 1999. For some people, massive changes happen quickly. For me, I am still learning about all the gifts God has in store for me. It's a process, removing yourself from the worldly things and completely submitting yourself to him, but I know you can do it!

Another good step could include finding a Bible-based church for your family. List some churches you want to visit and see if you find what you are looking for. Ask your friends at school or at work where they go. Talk to people you respect. Can't find one? Take twenty-five of your closest friends and show up to a new church one day. God will direct you! It's okay for you to have friends over and talk about Jesus. That's called a Bible study.

Enjoy your new beginning! I am very proud of you and will trust that you will find the encouragement you need during your daily walk with Him.

May God be with you always! Blessings my friend!

Christopher

About Christopher Milo

*C*hristopher Milo is a nationally renowned concert pianist and professional speaker. He has been fully trained in Life Skills and Resiliency with the Summit County Educational Service Center. He has spoken to over 100,000 students on the topics of leadership, bullying, suicide, teen pregnancy, drug and alcohol abuse, cutting and many other forms of self-harm. He embraces students who battle developmental disabilities, autism, cancer and diabetes.

Christopher continues to have ongoing relationships with local state hospitals and children's services, with partnerships at many Educational Service Centers within the State of Ohio. He is currently working with the Summit County Educational Service Center and the Summit County ADM Board to launch his 13 Messages from Milo (13MFM) Mentoring Program throughout the school system.

During a recent Leadership Conference with over 300 students in attendance, a teenager asked Christopher, "Why do you work with younger students?" He replied, "One day you may be balancing my checkbook when I am unable to see clearly, or you might be carrying my groceries when I lose the strength to do it myself. One day you might be the one making decisions for my community, or the country I fight for. If I can make even a small positive impact on our youth today, I will continue dedicating my life to doing just that!"

Educators have often asked why students are so eager to listen to someone like Christopher. With his unique program, students quickly and clearly see that Christopher is someone who cares and understands what they are going through. He uses real-life scenarios to drive the messages into the hearts and minds of people. He continues to bring out the truth by telling the truth. "13 Messages from Milo" creates a noninvasive environment that is welcoming to youth, where walls come down and relationships are made. A small idea in a small group becomes a life-changing opportunity for an entire student body.

Helpful Tools for the Home, Schools and Work.

I get asked the same questions everywhere I go. What are some things we can do to keep the "13 Messages from Milo" in front of us at all times?

No matter where you work, where you live or where you go to school, there is always room for motivation, encouragement and empowerment.

Schools:

- Make bulletin boards with the "13 Messages from Milo"
- Paint the beams in your school with one of the messages on each beam.
- Each week, apply one of the messages to your lesson plans.
- Ask students to use the message of the week at home. Every Friday, allow students a few minutes to discuss how they used that message at home or how they saw the message being misused.

Write down your ideas to implement the "13 Messages from Milo" in your school. I invite you to email me your ideas. I share information on christophermilo.com. Maybe your next great idea will show up for all to see!

Home:

- Put one of the "13 Messages from Milo" on the refrigerator each week.
- Discuss them weekly with the members of your family
- Make crafts using each message on construction paper and cut them out in different shapes.
- Make a collage
- Create a "Message Jar:" Every time someone in the house reports a wonderful way they used a message, put twenty-five cents or more in the jar. At the end of each week, treat the family to ice cream or something the entire family enjoys! You can choose your own denomination to put in the jar!

Work:

- One of the greatest ways to pump up your team and boost morale is to recognize them. If an employee was caught mentoring an employee in a positive way, write down "Be Positive" on a piece of paper with a sharpie marker. Have the employee hold it up and snap a picture of them.

Post the picture on your company website, around the office or in an email.

- Have an Employee of the Month program. To earn this title, you must implement the "13 Messages from Milo" all month long. The company could offer a gas card, gift certificate or even a cash appreciation award.

Create your own ideas here!_____

_____

_____

_____

_____

_____

_____

_____

Student Ideas And Committee Meetings

I wanted to give you an idea of what students come up with in the schools I visit. When we develop committees during Phase 2 and 3, we identify the needs of the school and break up the students into small groups. Each group has a new responsibility and works together to apply the "13 Messages from Milo" as well as aggressively addressing the needs they came up with.

Students create a name for their group and meet weekly to address the needs.

Examples from Students at Chestnut Intermediate School in North Olmsted, Ohio

GROUP 1
ISSUE: "Backbiters are cowards."
Students named the group:

S.S.R.C- Stanley Steamer Rumor Cleaner.

SOLUTIONS from Students:

1. Come together to discuss a solution.
2. Go and exercise.
3. Tell an adult or someone who is willing to listen and won't spread the rumor.
4. Kill 'em with kindness.
5. Keep your mouth closed if you're told a rumor. (Pretend you don't care or walk away.)
6. Tell somebody in a nice way to stop. (Remind them that they're spreading a rumor.)

6th Grade

<u>Group 2</u>
ISSUE: "Not accepting people's differences"

SOLUTIONS from Students:
As we talked in our small group, the words empathy and compassion came out. I also suggested that we all know what to say, but our focus needs to be centered around our actions. What are we actually going to do to implement change?

"Behave the way you would if your parents were right next to you."

Here are the brainstorming ideas from the group.

Find out the person's backstory

Try to figure out what people may be going through

Don't be a follower

Lead by example

Raise everybody up; don't bring them down

Focus on the pros and not the cons

Think before you say, type, or do

Don't hide behind the screen

Respect yourself

Build each other up

"Blowing out someone else's candle does not make yours shine any brighter."

GROUP 3

Issue: Students being mean to other students.

SOLUTIONS from Students:

*show empathy

*listen to what others are saying

*be more mature

*good sportsmanship

*From Confucius: "Treat others the way you want to be treated."

GROUP 4

Operation Beautiful!

SOLUTIONS from Students:

1.   Paint the parking lot spot ("teacher of the week")
2. Teacher appreciation day
3. Buy teachers something
4. Make cards for staff and put them in a binder
5. Another Mix Day
6. Sticky notes full of compliments
7. Day for teachers to play at recess
8. Special lunch for teachers
9. Teachers and students switch roles for the day
10. Positive quote each day
11. Decorate the classroom
12. All day recess full of games to get along with each other more
13. After school swim party
14. A teacher/student club

GROUP 5

ISSUE: Not Cooperating and Working Together 6th Grade

SOLUTIONS from Students:

1. LISTEN!

2. Each person gets a fair share.

3. Respect partners/opinions.

4. Find more opportunities to work together.

5. HELP EACH OTHER (and accept the help)!

6. Get to know each other.

7. Make decisions together as a whole group.

8. Include everyone.

9. Shut down bullying.

10. Encourage each other.

11. Solve problems.

12. Don't overreact.

13. Accept accidents for what they are.

14. Don't place blame.

15. Don't pick on and target people you dislike.

16. Mind your own business.

17. Don't interrupt or get others off-task just for fun.

18. Don't push others down; pick them up.

19. don't act like your better than everyone

20. Take turns.

21. Don't change for someone (unless for the better).

22. Don't judge people.

23. Cheer people up if they're sad.

24. Try something different.

Chestnut Intermediate School

You are invited!

For more information please visit www.christophermilo.com

and

listen to Christopher's album titled, "thirteen messages"

http://www.cdbaby.com/cd/christophermilo

Connect with Christopher!

LINKEDIN:

https://www.linkedin.com/in/christopher-milo86b85a32

FACEBOOK:

www.facebook.com/13messages

INSTAGRAM:

official_christopher_milo

YOU TUBE:

www.youtube.com/channel/UCnpVvSE5S4FWdoDjPC6xPYA

Thank you...

God

My wife Mary Beth, yes I'm coming to bed now!

My Family

Allen & Gwynne Ingram
www.athomemp.com

Saint Francis Xavier School

Steve Pelton
www.hchoices.com

Rev. Sheila Crawford at Shofar Ministries

Chestnut Intermediate School

Theresa Graves, Principal. Thank you for helping me "align" things and all the coffee! Oh Diggety!

All the students I have met along the way. You inspire me.

All the people over the years who treated me poorly and judged me who not only made me a better man but influenced this project! Jay Blum (Front/Back Cover Photos)

Five Fold Photography, LLC Cleveland, Ohio

and,

Jeremy Andrew Davis for all you have done for me over the years.

Wildfire Media Studios, LTD Canton, Ohio

Praise Jesus!

CPSIA information can be obtained
at www.ICGtesting.com
Printed in the USA
FFOW05n1031220717

9 781498 484039